1969

This book may be kept

FOURTEEN DAYS

A fine will be charged for each day the book is kept overtime.

SEP 23 75			
GAYLORD 142			PRINTED IN U.S.A.

ARGONAUT LIBRARY
OF ANTIQUITIES

ANCIENT GREEK DRESS

FIG. 1.—Cupbearer of Knossos.

FIGS. 2 and 3.—Snake Goddess and Votary. (*British School Annual*, IX., figs. 54 and 56.)

ANCIENT GREEK DRESS

A New Illustrated Edition Combining

GREEK DRESS by Ethel Abrahams
CHAPTERS ON GREEK DRESS by Lady Evans

Edited by

Marie Johnson, Ph.D.
Research Associate, Argonaut
Library of Antiquities

ARGONAUT, INC., PUBLISHERS
CHICAGO LIBRARY MCMLXIV

Library of Congress Catalog Card Number: *LC 64-23436*

EDITOR'S PREFACE

The study of Greek dress provides us with a more complete knowledge of the private and public lives of the ancient Greeks and new insight into their art and literature. Often the scenes depicted by ancient artists take on new meaning when one possesses a working knowledge of the costumes shown. Representations of ancient life remain in vase paintings, mosaics, reliefs and sculpture. These, plus literary references, provide us with our greatest knowledge of ancient apparel, for very few actual remnants of ancient Greek dress have survived the passing centuries.

From the simple austere lines of the clothing drawn by the archaic artist to the sophisticated and detailed representations of drapery and embroidery by those of the late Hellenistic age, the art historian can follow the evolution in style in art, and can successfully and accurately date the monuments of ancient art by proper application of his knowledge. The study of hair styles, jewelry and toilet articles also contributes to our knowledge of styles, artists and schools of Greek art. Historians can verify literary evidence by using these works of art as dated evidence and often is able to develop original historical theories by this method. That knowledge of Greek dress is helpful to the designer and archaeologist goes without saying.

While histories, handbooks and studies on Greek art and civilization contain bibliographical references to every phase of ancient life, the entries concerning the dress of the people are inevitably scarce. There are many valuable works on the absence of clothing and on specific apparel such as warrior's armor, but the dress of the average citizen has been less amply theated, not due to a lack of interest, but because the subject has been so thoroughly covered by three women of the twentieth century, Lady Evans and Miss Abrahams in the English language and Professor Margarete Bieber in German. Since the two books of the first two authors have little duplication they have been combined in this new edition to provide the most comprehensive reference book in English.

A number of new illustrations have been added, many of which were previously mentioned by the authors but not shown. My thanks are due to Mr. Al. Oikonomides who so kindly permitted me to use several photographs of unpublished antiquities from a work in preparation for the Chicago Natural History Museum. The original figures and plates have been incorporated into the new plates and the new list of illustrations should eliminate any problems which might have resulted from so rearranging the illustrations of the two books. The figure numbers are unchanged; the new illustrations are numbered with Roman numerals. The pagination of each book is unchanged for reference purposes.

Finally, a select bibliography has been added which, when combined with those of the originals, provides a relatively complete reference list on the subject of the dress of the ancient Greeks.

MARIE JOHNSON

Chicago, Illinois
June, 1964

SELECT BIBLIOGRAPHY

Barker, A. W., "Costumes of Athenian Women," in *AJA* 26, 1922 (no. 4).

Bieber, Margarete, "The Copies of the Herculaneum Women," in *Proc. Americ. Philosophical Society* 106, 1962, pp. 111-134.

——, *Entwicklungsgeschichte der Griechischen Tracht*, Berlin 1934.

——, *Griechische Kleidung*. Berlin 1928.

——, "Roman Men in Greek Himation (Romani Palliati)" in *Proc. Amer. Philosophical Society* 103, 1959, pp. 374-417.

——, *The Sculpture of the Hellenistic Age*. Rev. ed. New York 1960.

British Museum, A Guide to the Exhibition Illustrating Greek and Roman Life, London 1929. (*Dress and Toilet*, pp. 116-132).

Evans, Mary, *Costume Throughout the Ages*, London 1938.

Gardner, Percy, *A Grammar of Greek Art*, London 1908. (Chapter IV, *Dress and Drapery*, pp. 41-54).

Gulick, C. B., *Life of the Ancient Greeks*, New York 1911.

Houston, M. G., *Ancient Greek, Roman and Byzantine Costume*, London 1920.

Johnston. H. W., *Private Life of the Romans*, New York 1903

Metropolitan Museum, The Daily Life of the Greeks and Romans. New York 1924.

Picard-Schmitter, "Sur la chlamide de Demetrios Poliorcetes," in *Revue Archeologique* 46, 1955, pp. 17 ff.

Richter, G.M.A., "Silk in Greece," in *AJA* 33, 1929, pp. 27 :,

——, *A Handbook of Greek Art*, 2nd ed. London 1960. (Chapter XIII, *Textiles*, pp. 369-372, 397-398).

Schaefer, H., "Hellenistic Textiles in Northern Mongolia," in *AJA* 47, 1943, pp. 266 ff.

Tucker, T. G., *Life in Ancient Athens*, New York 1907.

Wace, A. J. B. & Lady Evans, "Dress," in Whibley's *Companion to Greek Studies* 4th ed. 1931, pp. 668-679.

Wilson, Lillian M., *The Clothing of the Ancient Romans*, Baltimore 1938.

——, *The Roman Toga*, Baltimore 1924.

Zora, P., *Cretan and Mycenaean Vogue and Dress*, Diss, Athens 1959 (in Greek).

CONTENTS

(*Note*: The pagination of *Greek Dress* by Ethel Abrahams
ends with 134, and begins anew in *Chapters on Greek
Dress* by Lady Evans.)

KEY TO PLATES

The plates of the two original books have been incorporated into the 52 plates of this edition, together with 39 new illustrations which are designated by Roman numerals. The plates from *Greek Dress* by Ethel Abrahams may be found in plates A-Z, AA-BB, while those from *Greek Dress* by Lady Evans are in plates MM-VV. The list below indicates the arrangement of these figures in the plates. For listings of the figures in greater detail see List of Illustrations in Abrahams, pages xix-xx, in Evans, pages v-x and List of New Illustrations (NI) below.

PLATE		PLATE	
A	Fig. 1	U	Figs. 39 & 40
B	Figs. 2 & 3	V	Figs. 41, a-c
C	Fig. 4	W	Figs. 43, a-b & 48, a-c
D	Fig. 5	X	Figs. 52, a-b & 53, a-b
E	Figs. 20 & 21	Y	Figs. 36 & 38
F	Figs. 22 & i	Z	Figs. 42, a-d
G	Figs. 23 & 25	AA	Figs. 45, a-l
H	Fig. 28	BB	Figs. 46, a-j
I	Fig. 7, a-c & 29	CC-JJ, KK-LL	Figs. iv-xxii, xxvii-xxviii (See NI)
J	Fig. 10	MM	Fig. 9
K	Figs. 11 & 37	NN	Fig. 10
L	Figs. 12 & 14	OO	Fig. 25
M	Fig. 13	PP	Figs. 17, 32 & 43
N	Figs. 15 & 16	RR	Fig. 35
O	Fig. 18	SS	Fig. 36
P	Fig. 19	TT	Fig. 38
Q	Fig. 27	UU	Fig. 52
R	Figs. 31 & 32	VV	Fig. 70
S	Figs. 34, a-b	WW-ZZ	Figs. xxix-xxxvii (See NI)
T	Fig. 35		

LIST OF NEW ILLUSTRATIONS

A-Abrahams *E*-Evans. Plates A-D in *A* pp. ii and xii; E-H in *A* between pp. 54-55; I-X in *A* between pp. 72-73; Y-Z, AA-BB in *A* between pp. 112-113. CC-JJ between *A* and *E*. KK-ZZ in *E* between pp. 50-51.

Plate / Page	
F	Fig. i Detail from an Attic kylix (ca. 440 B.C.), British Museum.
114	Fig. ii. Scene from an Attic kylix (ca. 440 B.C,), British Museum.
127	Fig. iii. Detail from scene on red-figured pyxis (toilet box). (ca. 470 B.C.) British Museum. Sleeveless Dorian chiton.
CC	Fig. iv. Black-figured Attic lekythos (ca. 550 B.C.) New York Metropolitan Museum of Art. Women weaving cloth.
DD	Fig. v. Black-figured Attic neck-amphora (ca. 540 B.C,) New York Metropolitan Museum of Art. Attic dress of man. woman and child.
	Fig. vi. Black-figured Attic amphora (ca. 540 B.C,) New York Metropolitan Museum of Art. Maidens in Attic chitons of mid-sixth c. B.C. and nude youths watching the hero

GREEK DRESS

A STUDY OF THE COSTUMES WORN IN
ANCIENT GREECE, FROM PRE-HELLENIC
TIMES TO THE HELLENISTIC AGE

BY ETHEL B. ABRAHAMS, M.A.

a

PLATE C

PLATE D

FIG. 4.—Fresco of a Dancing Girl.

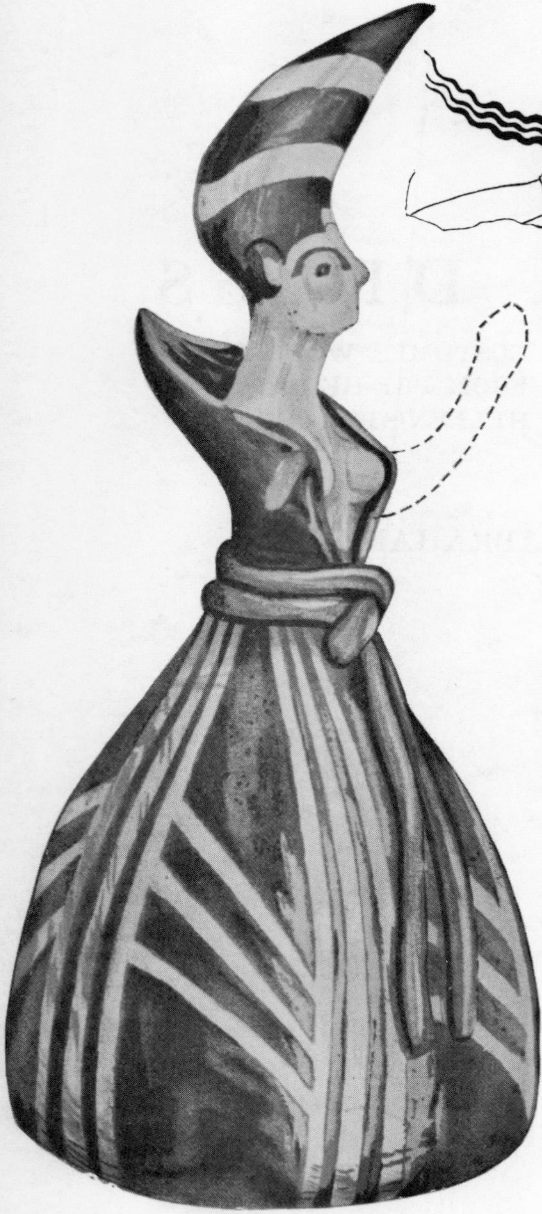

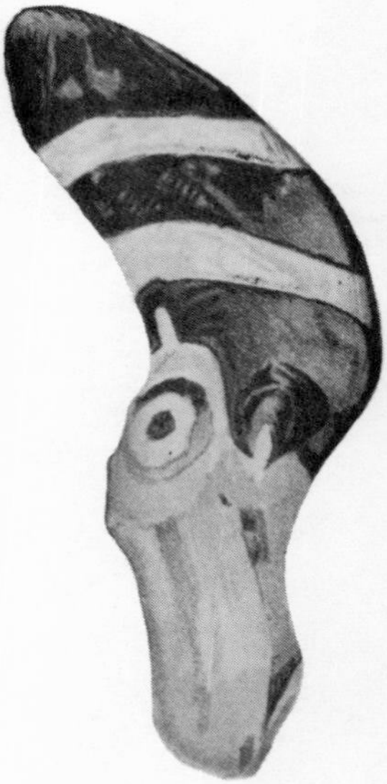

FIG. 5.—Statuette from Petsofa.

PREFACE

THE object of this book is to give a continuous account of the dress worn by the people inhabiting Greek lands, from the earliest times of which we have any record down to the Hellenistic age. The first chapter stands somewhat apart from the rest, since it deals with the costume of the race which occupied the Ægean shores before the real Hellenic races arrived on the scene, and of which we have abundant remains in Crete and elsewhere within the Ægean area. The remains found at Mycenæ, Tiryns, and other so-called Mycenæan sites, seem to be the last efforts of this dying civilization, which was replaced in the period of invasion and conquest recorded in the Homeric poems. I have been unable to trace any continuous development from the dress of this pre-Hellenic people to that of classic Greece, and the marked difference in the type of costume between the two periods bears out the theory of a difference of race.

I have endeavoured to show that the dress described in the Homeric poems is of the same type as the dress of classic Greece, and of this I have traced the historic development, classifying it into two main divisions, namely, Doric and Ionic. The simple and severe Doric dress contrasts with the more luxurious costume of the Ionian Greeks, although there are many instances, from the fifth century and onwards, in which the two styles are blended. I have noted also the elements which probably came in from Northern Greece; these are chiefly the chlamys and petasos.

The bulk of the following pages constituted a thesis approved for the degree of Master of Arts in the University of London. In revising the work for the press, however, some alterations and additions have been made. The chief of these is the addition of the section on the toilet; the illustrations have been carefully selected from extant monuments.

My sources for the chapter on pre-Hellenic dress have been mainly the finds of Mr A. J. Evans at Knossos, which I had the opportunity of seeing in the Candia Museum; these have been supplemented by the figures found at Petsofa, in Crete, and by various Mycenæan objects, notably rings and gems. The papers published by Mr Evans and Mr J. L. Myres in the *British School Annual* have been of very great value.

For the chapter on Homeric dress, my chief authority has been the poems themselves; in the absence of contemporary monuments, I have used the François vase to illustrate this section, since the figures upon it seem to tally most closely with the descriptions of dress found in the poems. Of modern literary authorities, the most valuable has been Studniczka's *Beiträge zur Geschichte der Altgriechischen Tracht*.

For the dress of the classical period, the evidence from extant art is abundant, and I have based my study chiefly upon it. Sculpture and vase-paintings have furnished the majority of my illustrations. I have noted many references to dress scattered up and down the ancient authors, and a passage from the fifth book of Herodotus has furnished a starting-point for the classification into Doric and Ionic dress.

My theory as to the shape and "cut" of the himation worn by the archaic ladies in the Acropolis Museum at Athens is, I think, a new one; it is based on a very careful examination of the statues, supplemented by some practical experiments in draping a living model.

For the sections on head-dress, materials, and footgear, I have referred to passages in ancient literature, and have used extant remains for illustrations, chiefly vase-paintings; except in the case of materials, for which I have cited the actual fragments of fabric found in Greek tombs at Kertch, in the Crimea.

In describing individual garments, I have in each case suggested dimensions and given diagrams, which, it is hoped, may be of practical use to those who wish to make Greek dresses for themselves.

Throughout the work, in addition to ancient

b

authorities, I have consulted the various articles in the current classical dictionaries. These include Pauly-Wissowa's *Real-Encyclopädie*, Daremberg and Saglio's *Dictionnaire des Antiquités grecques et romaines*, Smith's *Dictionary of Greek and Roman Antiquities*, Gardner and Jevons' *Manual of Greek Antiquities*, and the *Companion to Greek Studies*. Other works, to which single references have been made, are mentioned in the footnotes.

In addition to written authorities, I have received personal help from several scholars and friends, to whom I should like to express my thanks.

In the first place, I should like to acknowledge my indebtedness to the Reid Trustees of Bedford College, who elected me to a Fellowship in 1905, which enabled me to work for my second degree, and to spend some months in Greece as a student of the British School at Athens.

The suggestion that a thesis on the subject of Greek Dress might be of some value beyond getting me a degree, was due to Mr A. B. Cook, of Cambridge, under whom I had already worked for three years at Bedford College, and whose constant readiness to stimulate my leanings towards Archæology encouraged me to continue my studies in that direction. Mr Cook very kindly read this work in manuscript for me, and gave me the benefit of his criticisms. I owe a very great deal, also, to Professor Ernest Gardner, of University College, London, whose M.A. courses I attended regularly for two years, and from whom I constantly received help and guidance.

While in Athens, I devoted my attention chiefly to the dress of the archaic statues in the Acropolis Museum, and had the opportunity of discussing this subject with Mr R. C. Bosanquet, then director of the British School. I must also thank Herr Fritz Röhrig, the German sculptor, who placed his studio in Athens at my disposal, and procured a model for me, for the purpose of making my first experiments in reproducing the archaic style of draping the himation.

Special acknowledgments are due to Mr A. J. Evans, Mr J. L. Myres, and the Committee of the British School at Athens, for their courtesy in allowing me to reproduce subjects published by them in the *British School Annual;* to the Trustees of the British Museum, for permission to secure photographs of objects in the Museum for publication; to Mr Cecil Smith, for giving me free access to the library of the Department of Antiquities; and, particularly, to Mr H. B. Walters, who went through the illustrations with me, and greatly facilitated the task of securing suitable ones.

Lastly, my grateful thanks are due to Mr John Murray, for undertaking to publish the book, and to Mr A. H. Hallam Murray, for his constant courtesy and assistance during the progress of the work of publication.

E. B. A.

CONTENTS

LIST OF ILLUSTRATIONS

GREEK DRESS

I

INTRODUCTION

PRE-HELLENIC

In seeking to conjure up a vivid picture of the life of an ancient people, it is the task of the archæologist to neglect no point that can in any way throw light on the manners and customs which that people practised from day to day, both in the exercise of their public duties and in the privacy of their own homes.

Just as the habits and dress of an individual frequently give a true impression of his character and type of mind, so the salient characteristics of a nation are reflected in the external details of their manners and their costume. In making a careful study of the Greeks, therefore, whose innate feeling for beauty was part of their very being, and whose sense of the fitness of things rarely if ever played them false, we shall expect to find our efforts amply repaid, both by the satisfaction given to the æsthetic sense and by the knowledge we

A

shall have gained of the development of the national character. The study of costume has, moreover, an ethnological significance which in itself justifies a detailed investigation of the subject.

Professor Ridgeway, in *The Early Age of Greece*, has pointed out that the civilization reflected in the Homeric poems differs in many essential points from that which is revealed by the monuments found at Mycenæan sites on the mainland of Greece and in the Ægean islands. Confirmation has since been added to his convincing arguments by the discoveries of Mr Arthur Evans in Crete, which prove that the so-called Mycenæan remains were but the last efforts of a dying civilization which stretched back at least as far as the third millennium before our era. The culture revealed by the excavations at Knossos and other sites in Crete presents a striking contrast to that of the Greeks of the classic period; whereas the state of society described in the Homeric poems seems to contain analogies with both periods.

The palace of Alcinous and the house of Odysseus, as described in the *Odyssey*, correspond in plan to the palace of Mycenæ excavated by the Greek Archæological Society in 1886, which undoubtedly belongs to the older stratum of civilization;[1] on the other hand, the methods of dis-

[1] J. L. Myres, *Journal of Hellenic Studies*, vol. xx. Cp. also, for general principles of ground plan, "The Palace at Knossos," *British School Annual*, VIII.

posing of the dead, and the underlying principles
of costume, are utterly different in the two cases.
The Homeric heroes burn their dead, whereas the
remains found in Mycenæan graves prove that in
the state of society to which they belong burial
was the common method of disposing of the dead.
The difference in costume is equally striking; the
women's dress, illustrated by the Mycenæan gems
and the wall-paintings and faïence statuettes from
Knossos, consists of elaborately made garments,
with tight jackets fitting closely to the figures at
the waist, and full and frequently flounced skirts;
there is no indication of fastening by means of
brooches or fibulæ. In Homer the brooch is
almost invariably mentioned as an essential detail
of female costume, and the garments described are
of a simple character, and such that they can be
spread out and used for other purposes. For
example, Aphrodite, when protecting Æneas from
his assailants, shields him from their weapons by
drawing a fold of her peplos over him (*Iliad*, v.,
315); and again, at the funeral rites of Hector, the
body is covered, πορφυρέοις πέπλοισι μαλακοῖσιν (*Iliad*,
xxiv., 796), "with soft purple robes."

The contrast between the forms of dress represented in Mycenæan art and in the Homeric
poems can only be explained by supposing that
there is a difference in race between the two
peoples, and that the older civilization was almost
entirely swept away by a great series of invasions
carried out by men of a different race. The

Homeric dress is closely akin to that of the Greeks
of the classic period, whereas that represented on
Mycenæan rings and gems belongs, as will be
shown later, to the stratum of civilization revealed
by the Cretan excavations.[1] We must suppose,
then, that the Homeric heroes belonged to the
invading race, which was full of youthful vigour
and succeeded in superimposing its manners and
customs upon those of the older, decadent society,
and in finally ousting the older inhabitants from
their homes altogether. The process was one
which must have lasted over some centuries, and
it is probable that the Homeric poems were composed whilst it was still incomplete, and that the
siege of Troy represents one incident in the long
wars which were waged between the two peoples.
This view accounts for the fact that the Homeric
house belongs to the older civilization, while the
costume is that of the later. The invaders, having
conquered or driven out the inhabitants, finding
their houses strongly built and luxuriously
decorated, would refrain from destroying them
and settle themselves peacefully and comfortably
there, naturally retaining their own style of dress
and customs of disposing of their dead. Any new
houses built after their settlement would be constructed after their own plans, and so the Homeric
house would gradually give place to the Hellenic.
The absence of brooches and fibulæ from the graves
on the Acropolis of Mycenæ, and their presence in

---

[1] Cp. Busolt, *Griechische Geschichte*, vol. i., 2nd ed., chap. i.

those of the lower city, adds confirmation to this
theory. The Acropolis graves are earlier than the
others, which in all probability belong to the time
when the invaders had already imposed some of
their characteristic customs upon their predecessors
at Mycenæ and elsewhere in Greece. The use of
the fibula is common to the early peoples of
Central Europe, from which region it must have
been introduced by the Achæan invaders into
Greece.[1]

The earliest remains found on Greek soil are
those which have been unearthed by Mr A. J.
Evans, in his series of excavations at Knossos, in
Crete. They represent earlier stages of that
civilization which has hitherto been known as
Mycenæan. The costume revealed by the art of
this pre-Hellenic age forms a study in itself, since
it presents a striking contrast to that of the classic
period in Greece, and also to that of contemporary
Asiatic peoples. The costume of the men is
simple; when not entirely nude, they wear sometimes a waist-cloth rolled round a girdle, with a
loose end hanging down like an apron in front;[2]
in a lead statuette of the same period found near
Abbia, in Laconia, the waist-cloth appears to take
the form of a triangular piece of material wrapped
round the girdle, the apex of the triangle being
drawn up between the legs and tucked into the

[1] Ridgeway, *Early Age of Greece*, chap. viii.; S. Müller, *Urgeschichte Europas*, pp. 95, 96.

[2] Fig. 1, Cupbearer of Knossos. Cp. also, Vaphio Cup, gems,
Perrot and Chipiez, VI., 426. 21.

belt in front. In some terra-cotta figurines from Petsofa,[1] a third garment appears, consisting of a rectangular piece of material with the long side tucked into the belt all round and the short sides hanging down perpendicularly in front. In the later Mycenæan period, the garment takes the form of short breeches reaching half-way down the thigh. These are probably a development from the earlier waist-cloth.[2]

In most cases the upper part of the body appears to be quite bare, but in some instances a line is drawn at the neck and wrists which may indicate the edges of a close-fitting, long-sleeved tunic. It is more probable, however, that these lines are meant to represent a necklace and bracelets, such as have been found in considerable numbers in Mycenæan graves. On a siege scene represented on a fragment of a silver vase from Mycenæ,[3] the majority of the fighting warriors are represented quite nude; but in one case (at the lower right-hand corner) a tunic and head-dress are worn; but in this instance the tunic has sleeves reaching only half-way to the elbow, as is also the case with the inhabitants, who are watching the progress of the battle from behind the city wall; two figures, which appear to be just leaving the city, wear square cloaks fastened on the right shoulder and leaving both arms free; they do not appear to

[1] *British School Annual*, IX., pls. ix. and x.
[2] Dagger blade from Mycenæ. Perrot and Chipiez, VI., pl. xviii., 3.
[3] Perrot and Chipiez, VI., fig. 365.

be fighting, and probably represent heralds about to make some proposal to the enemy. The covering here described as a cloak has been regarded as representing an oblong shield (ἠύτε πύργος); but in view of the fact that the men carry no weapons and that both arms are exposed, it seems more reasonable to suppose that a mantle is intended. The warriors in front are fighting without protection; and if any shield were represented, we should expect it to be of the usual Mycenæan shape, which appears as a decoration on the upper left-hand corner of the fragment. A fragment of a wall-painting from Mycenæ represents a warrior wearing a short-sleeved tunic and having a double bracelet at the wrist; it appears, then, that when the pre-Hellenic man wore a tunic, it was not furnished with long sleeves, and even when his clothing was of the scantiest possible nature, he was not far enough removed from primitive barbarism to prevent his adorning his person with bracelet and necklace.

The indication of some kind of footgear is frequent: it is represented on the Vaphio cups; and on a wall-painting from Tiryns depicting the capture of a bull, it takes the form of pointed shoes turned up at the toes and fastened by a series of bands above the ankles. Such pointed shoes were common to the Assyrians and the Hittites, and are worn to this day by Greeks and Turks, and frequently also in other rocky countries.[1]

In the wall-painting from Tiryns, and on a

---

[1] The characteristic Cretan boots may possibly be a direct survival.

Mycenæan intaglio (Perrot and Chipiez, VI., 426. 21), a number of bands is indicated just below the knee. Possibly the boots were fastened by leather laces crossed round the legs and then passed two or three times round under the knees. At present these bands have only been found in cases where the wearer is engaged in some violent occupation, such as the bull-taming scene; it has been suggested that they represent a leather thong wound round the knees to act as a protection; on stony ground some such guard would be necessary.

The head-dress, of conical shape, finished by a button or flattened knob on the top, represents a helmet, made sometimes probably of metal, as was the case in Assyria, but in some cases certainly of felt or leather, covered with rows of overlapping boar's tusks, turned alternately in opposite directions. A large number of boar's tusks were found by Dr Schliemann[1] at Mycenæ, flattened on one side and with several holes in them, which obviously served to fasten them to some object; such a helmet is to be seen in an ivory fragment from Mycenæ,[2] and would exactly correspond to that described in *Iliad*, X., 261.

ἀμφὶ δ' οἱ κυνέην κεφαλῆφιν ἔθηκεν
ῥινοῦ ποιητήν· πολέσιν δ' ἔντοσθεν ἱμᾶσιν
ἐντέτατο στερεῶς, ἔκτοσθε δὲ λευκοὶ ὀδόντες
ἀργιοδόντος ὑός. Θαμέες ἔχον ἔνθα καὶ ἔνθα
εὖ καὶ ἐπισταμένως.

---

[1] Schliemann, *Mycenæ*, pp. 272, 273.
[2] Perrot and Chipiez, VI., fig. 380; Ἐφήμερις Ἀρχαιολογική, 1888, pl. viii.

"And about his head he set a helmet made of leather; and inside it was stiffly wrought with many thongs, and outside the white teeth of a boar with shining tusks were set close together, this way and that, well and cunningly arranged."

In some cases the helmet presents a strikingly Egyptian appearance, and may quite possibly have been derived from Egypt; evidence of direct intercourse between the Cretans and Egyptians is not wanting; indeed the clearest representation of the costume of the pre-Hellenic inhabitants of the Ægean shores is to be found on an Egyptian tomb fresco,[1] where the Kefts are depicted bringing vases as tribute to the Egyptian monarch, their costume is identical with that of the cupbearer from the Knossian fresco, and they are carrying vessels of the same shapes as many which have been found in Crete and on other Mycenæan sites. It has been pointed out by Mr H. R. Hall[2] that the Keftiu were the people of the Ægean islands, including Crete, and that sometimes the name was applied exclusively to the Cretans. The Keftiu were formerly mistaken for Phœnicians; but their whole appearance and costume on the Egyptian fresco is utterly unlike anything Phœnician; so we are quite justified in considering that they represent the Cretans faithfully as they appeared to the Egyptians, especially in view of their similarity to the cup-

---

[1] Perrot and Chipiez, III., fig. 303.
[2] *British School Annual*, IX., "Keftiu and the Peoples of the Sea."

bearer of the fresco at Knossos, a native product
of Cretan art.

A striking analogy to the pre-Hellenic male
costume is to be observed in the Etruscan wall-
paintings from the tombs at Corneto, now in the
British Museum. The waist-cloth, shoes, and head-
dress are there represented in a form almost identical
with that found in Mycenæan art. So little is
known of the origin of the Etruscans, that it is
difficult to say whether this similarity of dress
indicates any racial connection between the two
peoples ; it is interesting to note that among ancient
authorities Hellanicus of Lesbos states that the
Etruscans were of Pelasgian origin, and modern
writers have claimed a Pelasgian origin for the
Cretans ; there is not sufficient evidence forthcoming at present to determine whether they are
right or wrong ; but in any case, it is not improbable
that both the Etruscans and the Cretans were
branches of a common civilization, which spread
itself all round the shores of the Mediterranean Sea
in pre-Hellenic times, and that the Etruscans
maintained some of their early characteristics down
to a later date than other peoples of the same
race.[1]

Turning to the female costume of the pre-
Hellenic age, we find we have something far more
complicated to deal with. The same style of dress
is found on the early faïence figures from Knossos

[1] Daremberg and Saglio, *Dictionnaire des Antiquités*, s.v.
"Etrusci."

and Petsofa, and extends right on until quite late Mycenæan times.

It consists of a short-sleeved jacket, fitting closely to the figure, and a full skirt, standing out round the feet in a manner suggestive of the hoops of the early Victorian age. The juncture of the two garments is hidden by a thick double girdle worn round the waist, which is pinched into the smallest possible compass.

The snake goddess and her votary[1] from Knossos have, in addition, a kind of apron reaching almost to the knees in front and behind, and rising to the hips at the sides. The costume is completed by the addition of a high hat or turban.

Looking at the snake goddess more in detail, we find that the jacket is cut away into a V-shape from the neck to the waist, leaving both the breasts quite bare ; the two edges are laced across below the breast, the laces being fastened in a series of bows. The jacket is covered with an elaborate volute pattern, the apron with spots and bordered with a "guilloche." The horizontal lines on the skirt probably represent stripes in the material, the edge being ornamented with a reticulated band. The girdle of the goddess is composed of two snakes intertwined. The head-dress here consists of a high turban, probably made of cloth or linen wound round some kind of framework. The principle of the costume is always the same, though the fashions vary considerably in detail : for example, the skirt of

[1] Figs. 2 and 3 from *British School Annual*, IX.

the votary is composed of a series of seven flounces,
one above the other, the lower edge in each case
just covering the upper edge of the flounce below,
the whole being probably sewn on to a foundation.
On a fresco[1] representing a lady dancing, the skirt
seems to consist of three such flounces. On the
same figure the breast is not left bare, but a
chemisette seems to be worn under the jacket,
possibly made of some fine linen material, the edge
of which is distinctly indicated at the neck.   In one
of the statuettes from Petsofa[2] the jacket terminates
at the back in a high "Medici" collar, and in
another fresco, from Knossos, a high sash appears
on the back, the loop reaching to the nape of the
neck, and the fringed edge hanging down to the
waist; at first sight this sash recalls the Japanese
"Obi."[3] The millinery of the Cretan ladies, as
illustrated by the terra-cotta fragments from Petsofa,
exhibits an abundant variety of styles. The hat
seems to have consisted of a flat, circular, or oval
piece of material pinched up into any shape to suit
the taste of the wearer; sometimes it is fastened
down towards the nape of the neck, and curves
round the head, rising high up in front over the
face; in one case[4] the brim has a wavy edge and is
trimmed with rosettes underneath; frequently it is

---

[1] Fig. 4, only a very small fragment of the skirt remains; but the
painting has been restored. Reproduced from the *British School
Annual*, VIII., fig. 28.

[2] Fig. 5 from *British School Annual*, IX., pl. viii.

[3] The large sash worn over the "Kimono" and tied rather high up
at the back.   [4] *British School Annual*, IX., pls. xi. and xii.

done up into a large "toque" shape, narrowing to a point in front; this form occurs also on late Mycenæan terra-cottas.

On none of the examples of costume quoted above is there any indication of fastening; the garments are obviously constructed by an elaborate system of sewing, but the means by which they were held in place on the figure is not represented, except in the case of the bodices of the goddess and her votary, which are laced across by cords. The use of fibulæ is nowhere indicated in art; and no fibulæ have been found, except in the later Mycenæan graves, which in all probability belong to the Achæan civilization introduced into Greece by the invasions from Central Europe.[1] A fragmentary hand from Petsofa has a bracelet represented in white paint, which is clearly fastened by means of a button and loop; since this method of fastening was known to the Cretans, it is probable that the ladies' skirts were fastened at the waist by buttons and loops, the fastening being concealed by the belt, as is the case with the modern blouse and skirt costume.

It has been pointed out by Mr J. L. Myres[2] that this jacket and apron type of dress is commonly worn at the present day by the peasants of the mountainous districts of Europe, chiefly in Italy, Switzerland, the Tyrol, Norway, and the Pyrenees. In Norway and Switzerland, moreover, we find the

---

[1] On "fibulæ," see Sophus Müller, *Urgeschichte Europas*, p. 95. O. Montelius, *Civilization of Sweden in Heathen Times*.

[2] *British School Annual*, IX.

addition of a fan-like head-dress analogous to that represented in Minoan art. The appearance of the same kind of costume in Crete in the third millennium before our era merely serves to show that the type of dress need not necessarily be a modern development, but may possibly claim greater antiquity than has hitherto been supposed. The question of survival in the Ægean is interesting; as late as Tournefort's[1] time, the inhabitants of some of the islands—for example, Mycone—appear to have worn a dress composed of a tight jacket and flounced skirt, with the addition of some Turkish elements; in the remoter islands there is a possibility—but it is little more than a possibility —that this may be a case of survival; in any case, the type seems to have disappeared in the eighteenth or early nineteenth century.[2]

[1] Tournefort, I., 109.

[2] See also, Choiseul-Gouffier, *Voyage pittoresque de la Grèce*, Paris, 1809, where the women of the islands are represented wearing a tight corslet over a chemisette. A high head-dress, not unlike that of the Petsofa statuettes, was commonly worn by the island women as late as the eighteenth century.

II

HOMERIC

TURNING to the various passages in the Homeric poems which refer to dress, we find that there is very little likelihood that they can be intended to describe the kind of costume dealt with above under the name of "Pre-Hellenic Dress." The words used, and the accounts of the process of dressing, have no meaning, unless we suppose them to refer to the draped type of costume as opposed both to the close-fitting jacket type and to the dressing-gown type, consisting of a loose-sleeved garment opening down the front. The question of the kind of dress actually worn by the Trojan and Achæan heroes is not one to be entered into here; possibly it may have been the same as that reflected in the art of the Minoan and Mycenæan peoples; indeed, if the Trojans represent the older race which inhabited the shores of the Ægean, and the Achæans the invaders who came down upon them from the north, there is every probability that the former wore the pre-Hellenic dress, and the latter introduced the new Hellenic draped type. The use of the epithets βαθύκολπος and βαθύζωνος, "deep - bosomed" and "deep-girdled," in the Homeric poems perhaps has some bearing on this point. Referring respectively to the deep hollow between the breasts and to the girdle cutting deep into the figure, they might well be applied to the wasp-waisted ladies of Knossos. It is significant to notice that βαθύκολπος is used only of Trojan women,[1] βαθύζωνος only of barbarian captives;[2] possibly the poet may be unconsciously referring to the difference between the dress of the older race and that of their Achæan conquerors.

However that may be, in most cases Homer ascribes the same kind of costume to Achæans and Trojans alike; he is singing of deeds that happened many years, perhaps even two or three centuries, before his day, and being no archæologist, he imagines his heroes to have dressed as his own contemporaries did; he is acting no differently from the Italian masters, who painted their Madonnas in mediæval costume.

We find in Homer many differences in the nomenclature used when speaking of men's and women's dresses respectively. The words χιτών and χλαῖνα are applied exclusively to men's costume, πέπλος and κρήδεμνον exclusively to women's, whereas the word φᾶρος is the only one used indifferently for either; both men and women alike fasten their garments with brooches or pins of some kind (περόνη, ἐνετή) and with girdles (ζώνη, ζωστήρ). Many of the words applied to articles of wearing-apparel

---

[1] Iliad, 18. 122, 389, 24. 215.   [2] Ibid., 9. 594; Odyssey, 3. 154.

are also used to signify coverings for beds, seats, etc. : such are χλαῖνα, ῥήγεα, πέπλος, φᾶρος; the last is used also of sails and of the shroud of Laertes.[1] This being the case, we must infer that they were not made-up garments, but large square or oblong pieces of material which could be used for other purposes besides clothing ; the Homeric dress, therefore, must belong to the draped type rather than to any other.

The men's dress in Homer regularly consists of two pieces—the χιτών, or undergarment, and a cloak called variously χλαῖνα, φᾶρος, or, in one case, λώπη.[2] Warriors sometimes wore a skin instead of the mantle. For example, in *Iliad*, x., 22, Agamemnon is described as putting on a lion's skin, and a few lines further on Menelaus appears wearing a dappled leopard's skin.

The description of the process of dressing in the *Iliad* is simple and straightforward. Agamemnon[3] awakes in the morning, and prepares to meet the assembly of the Achæans :

ἕζετο δ' ὀρθωθεὶς μαλακὸν δ' ἔνδυνε χιτῶνα
καλὸν νηγάτεον, περὶ δὲ μέγα βάλλετο φᾶρος·
πόσσι δ' ὑπὸ λιπαροῖσιν ἐδήσατο καλὰ πέδιλα,
ἀμφὶ δ' ἄρ' ὤμοισιν βάλετο ξίφος ἀργυρόηλον.

"He sat upright and drew on his soft tunic, fair and new, and threw around him his great cloak : and beneath his shining feet he bound fair sandals, and around his shoulders he slung his silver-studded sword."

[1] *Odyssey*, xix., 137.　　[2] *Ibid.*, xiii., 22.　　[3] *Iliad*, ii., 42.

C

The χιτών was apparently, then, a garment which could be drawn on (ἔνδυνε) while in a sitting position. No mention is made, either in this or other similar passages, of pins or girdle to fasten the χιτών, so we may infer that it was a rather narrow garment sewn up at the two sides, with openings left for the head and arms.

Studniczka [1] gives a diagram of such a garment, which he describes as a sack left open at the bottom,

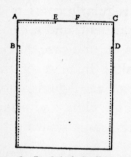

FIG. 6. Studniczka's Diagram. The dotted lines mark the seams, the spaces A B, C D, E F being left open for arms and head respectively.

with openings in the top and side-seams for head and arms.

The words ἐνδύνω, ἐκδύνω, are commonly used for "to put on" and "to take off" a χιτών, which seems to imply that the garment was drawn over the head; although occasionally περί is used with the simple verb δύνω instead of the compound ἐνδύνω.[2]   In no case is there any mention of pins or brooches in connection with the χιτών, so we are justified in inferring that it was a sewn garment; and in *Odyssey*, xxiv., 227, the χιτών of Laertes is actually described as sewn :

ῥυπόωντα δὲ ἔστο χιτῶνα
ῥαπτὸν ἀεικέλιον.

"He wore a sewn tunic, dirty and unseemly."

[1] *Beiträge zur Geschichte der altgriechischen Tracht*, p. 13.
[2] *Odyssey*, xv., 60.

As a rule, the χιτών was worn ungirdled, except when the wearer was engaged in vigorous action, when he is usually described as girding himself for the purpose. For example, in the *Odyssey*,[1] when Eumæus is going to slay pigs, he prepares himself by confining his χιτών with a girdle :

ὣς εἰπὼν ζωστῆρι θοῶς συνέεργε χιτῶνα.

Little mention is made in the Homeric poems of the length of the χιτών, but the distinguishing epithet of the Ionians is ἑλκεχιτῶνες—with trailing chitons—so that trailing garments were evidently customary only among the Ionians ; warriors while fighting and slaves occupied in active work would probably wear very short garments reaching only to the thigh, as they are to be seen on the earliest vase-paintings. The princes and elders of the people, engaged in peaceful pursuits, in all probability wore them reaching to the ankles. The word τερμίοεις, applied to the χιτών in *Odyssey*, xix., 242, is usually taken to mean "reaching to the feet," and to be equivalent to ποδήρης, used by later writers.

With regard to the material of which the χιτών was made, the word itself is connected with a Semitic root signifying linen ;[2] and from the various epithets applied to it in Homer, it is reasonable to infer that the garment was ordinarily made of that material. It is described as σιγαλόεις, "shining" or "glossy"; and although

[1] xiv. 72.
[2] Pauly-Wissowa, *Real Encyclopädie, s.v.* " χιτών," Studniczka, p. 15 f.

this particular epithet need mean no more than "dazzlingly clean," its comparison for softness and brightness with the skin of an onion[1] would hardly be very apt, if it were made of a stuff that did not present a very smooth surface; a hand-woven woollen material might possibly be called μαλακός, "soft," but could hardly be described as shining like the sun. Two passages in Homer show clearly that oil was used in the weaving of linen, which would have the effect of producing a shiny appearance. The maidens in the palace of Alcinous are described as weaving linen from which the oil runs off:

καιρουσσέων δ' ὀθονέων ἀπολείβεται ὑγρὸν ἔλαιον.

[*Odyssey*, vii., 107.]

"And from the close-woven linen the liquid oil runs off," and in *Iliad*, 596, the youths in the dancing place on the shield of Achilles are described as wearing χιτῶνας εὐννήτους, ἦκα στίλβοντας ἐλαίῳ, "well spun, shining softly with oil."

The epithet στρέπτος applied to the χιτών[2] requires comment; it was taken by Aristarchus, the grammarian, to mean a coat of chain mail. There is no evidence to show that such a piece of defensive armour was known to the early Greeks, and we find

---

[1] *Odyssey*, xix., 232:

τὸν δὲ χιτῶν' ἐνόησα περὶ χροΐ σιγαλόεντα
οἷόν τε κρομύοιο λοπὸν κατὰ ἰσχαλέοιο
τὼς μὲν ἔην μαλακός, λαμπρὸς δ' ἦν ἠέλιος ὥς.

"And I saw the shining tunic on his body, like the skin of a dried onion—so soft it was, and bright as the sun."

[2] *Iliad*, v., 113; xxi., 31.

no reference to it until Roman times; there is, therefore, no justification for the inference that στρεπτός χιτών in Homer means a coat of mail.

The word στρεπτός means primarily "twisted," and could be applied to a coarse kind of linen whose texture showed very clearly the separate threads of which it was woven; but other uses of the word in Homer, and the second of the two passages in which it is applied to a χιτών, suggest a different interpretation. In *Odyssey*, ii., 426, in the description of the rigging of a ship, the expression εὐστρέπτοισι βοεῦσιν occurs. The adjective here can very well retain its simple meaning—"well-twisted"; the noun can mean nothing else but "ropes of ox-hide"—that is to say, the whole expression will signify ropes made of well-twisted thongs of leather.

The passage referred to in the *Iliad* runs as follows :—

> δῆσε δ' ὀπίσσω χεῖρας εὐτμήτοισιν ἱμᾶσι
> τοὺς αὐτοὶ φορέεσκον ἐπὶ στρέπτοισι χιτῶσι.
>
> [*Iliad*, xxi., 30.]

The subject is the sacrifice of the twelve boys at the funeral of Patroclus.

Achilles bound their hands behind them with the well-cut thongs which they wore on their twisted chitons. The word ἱμᾶσι implies leather, and the only kind of chiton which would be likely to have leather thongs attached to it would be a jerkin made of leather, perhaps plaited in some way and fastened by means of leather laces. Such a garment might be worn in war under a metal breast-plate, or if very stoutly made might even serve as defensive armour, without the addition of any corslet; in any case, it would afford more protection than an ordinary linen chiton such as was worn by those engaged in the pursuits of peace.

Another garment worn by men is the ζῶμα, which appears at first sight to mean simply a girdle, but in one or two passages signifies something more. The word is obviously connected with the verb ζώννυμι, "to gird on," and means a "thing girt on." The word might well apply to a girdle, but it might also be used of anything put on round the waist, and so of a waist-cloth; there can be little doubt that it has this meaning in *Iliad*, xxiii., 683, where a description is being given of the preparations for a boxing match; and a few lines further on the participle ζωσαμένω, applied to the wrestlers, in all probability means putting on their waist-cloths. In other passages where the word occurs, its meaning is less obvious, although here too there is nothing to render the same interpretation impossible. In *Iliad*, iv., 186, a weapon is described as not inflicting a mortal wound:

εἰρύσατο ζωστήρ τε παναίολος ἠδ᾽ ὑπένερθεν
ζῶμά τε καὶ μίτρη, τὴν χαλκῆες κάμον ἄνδρες.

"But the shining belt checked it, and the waist-cloth beneath, and the kirtle which the coppersmiths fashioned."

Here the ζωστήρ and the μίτρη are obviously pieces of armour, and the ζῶμα is a garment worn under the ζωστήρ, and can very well bear the meaning of a waist-cloth. Such garments were worn at all periods; they formed the regular dress of the men of the pre-Hellenic age; they occur also on vases of the classical period.[1] There is no necessity, therefore, to suppose, as Studniczka does, that the word here is synonymous with χιτών. Studniczka supports his interpretation of this passage by another, *Odyssey*, xiv., 478 f., where Eumæus is describing to Odysseus an occasion when he and comrades had to sleep in the open air, and he felt the cold because he had foolishly left his cloak behind him, and had only his shield and ζῶμα φαεινόν. The expression could here maintain its signification of "waist-cloth"; only, the simple meaning is obscured by a phrase some five lines further on, when Eumæus continues:

οὐ γὰρ ἔχω χλαῖναν· παρὰ μ' ἤπαφε δαίμων
οἰοχίτων' ἔμεναι.

"I had no cloak: some god beguiled me to go with only a single garment."

The simple meaning of οἰοχίτων is, "wearing only a chiton," or under-garment; but without stretching the meaning of the expression very far, we can easily suppose its being applied to a man clad only in a waist-cloth; so that even here it is not necessary to suppose that ζῶμα is another word for χιτών.

[1] Cp. Fig. 7 (a); the human figure struggling with the Minotaur.

We must next consider the over-garment worn by the Homeric heroes, for which several words are used, the most common being χλαῖνα and φᾶρος.

The χλαῖνα was used not only as an article of dress, but also as a blanket to sleep under;[1] as a rug to cover couches and seats;[2] a constant epithet is οὔλη, so that its material was evidently woollen; and the adjectives ἀλεξάνεμος and ἀνεμοσκεπής, "warding off winds," show that it was worn for warmth, as a protection against cold winds.[3] It was thrown off for exercise or when speed in running was required.[4] The style in which the χλαῖνα was worn varied somewhat; the verbs regularly used for the act of putting it on are ἀμφιβάλλω and ἀμφιέννυμι, "to throw round"; περιβάλλω also occurs, and sometimes it is described as being placed ἐπ' ὤμοισι, "upon the shoulders"; for taking it off, ἀποβάλλω and ἀποτίθημι are used, and in one case ἐκδύνω occurs, though this word should more correctly be applied to the χιτών. The constant use of ἀμφί, "around," shows that the χλαῖνα was not a garment which was drawn on over the head, like the χιτών, but was a square or rectangular piece of material wrapped round the figure or laid over the shoulders. We read in Homer of the χλαῖνα ἁπλοΐς, "single cloak," and the χλαῖνα διπλῆ, "double cloak"; the former expression must mean a cloak worn single, without being folded over; such a garment might possibly be put on as the himation was in later time, one end

---

[1] *Odyssey*, iii., 349.
[2] *Ibid.*, xvii., 86.
[3] *Ibid.*, xiv., 522.
[4] *Iliad*, ii., 183.

being laid on the shoulder, so that the mass of the material hung down towards the back; this mass of material would then be drawn across the back under the arm which was then left exposed, and across the chest, and the end would be thrown over the shoulder towards the back. The garment could easily be drawn up so as to cover both arms if the temperature required greater warmth, or it might be worn over both shoulders like a shawl, without being doubled, and the frequent mention of the shoulders in connection with the χλαῖνα seem to point to this style as the most common.[1] The χλαῖνα διπλῆ is mentioned twice in Homer—once in the *Iliad* and once in the *Odyssey*; in both cases it is described as being fastened with a brooch:

ἀμφὶ δ' ἄρα χλαῖναν περονήσατο φοινικόεσσαν
διπλῆν ἐκταδίην.   [*Iliad*, x., 133.]

"And about him he fastened a purple cloak, doubled, with no folds."

χλαῖναν πορφυρέην οὐλὴν ἔχε δῖος 'Οδυσσεύς,
διπλῆν· αὐτὰρ οἱ περόνη χρυσοῖο τέτυκτο
αὐλοῖσιν διδύμοισι.   [*Odyssey*, xix., 225.]

"Goodly Odysseus had a purple cloak, woollen and doubled; and it had a brooch wrought of gold, with a double groove for the pins."

In these cases the χλαῖνα was obviously folded over double, though in what way is not expressly stated; if the garment consisted of a wide rect-

---

[1] See Fig. 7 (*a*), where the second figure from the right is represented wearing only the χλαῖνα ἁπλοῒς.

angular piece of material, it might be doubled along
its length horizontally and fastened with a brooch
on one shoulder, like Apollo's himation in the
Thasos relief.[1] This method, however, is not
found on the earliest vases, which, though not
contemporary with Homer, are yet the nearest
monumental evidence obtainable; moreover, the
additional expression, ἐκταδίην, seems to be against
this interpretation; the meaning of ἐκταδίην seems
to be "stretched out straight," and the word
could hardly be applied to a garment draped in
such a way as to fall in many folds; it is reasonable, therefore, to suppose that the χλαῖνα διπλῆ
consisted of a large square[2] of woollen material
folded along the diagonal, so that two opposite
corners lay on each other; it would be laid on the
shoulders so that these two corners hung down in
the middle of the back, no folds being formed
(ἐκταδίην), and the other two points hung down one
on each side of the front; a brooch would prevent
the cloak from slipping off the shoulders; this
shawl-like method of wearing the mantle is frequently represented on the black figured vases.[3]
The δίπτυχον λώπην, "double cloak," which Athena
wears, ἀμφ' ὤμοισι, when disguised as a shepherd,[4] is
probably a garment worn in this same fashion,

---

[1] E. A. Gardner, *Handbook of Greek Sculpture*, p. 128.

[2] Unless the garment were square, the diagonally opposite corners
would not coincide when folded corner to corner; they are invariably
represented on the vases as coinciding.

[3] Fig. 7 (*b*) is taken from the "François" vase.

[4] *Odyssey*, xiii., 223.

and the δίπλακες which Helen and Andromache are described as weaving in the *Iliad*[1] are perhaps intended for cloaks to be so worn.

The place of the χλαῖνα is frequently taken by the φᾶρος, constant epithets of which are καλὸν and μέγα, "fine" and "large," so that we may conclude that the φᾶρος was an ample and somewhat luxurious garment. The word is used not only for an article of wearing apparel, but also for the shroud of Laertes,[2] and for the sails of a ship,[3] so that Studniczka's conjecture that it was made of linen is probably right, and the difference of material probably constitutes the chief distinction between the φᾶρος and the χλαῖνα. The φᾶρος is several times described as "white" and "well-washed," and the epithets ἀργυφεόν, λέπτον, χαρίεν, "silvery," "fine," and "graceful," which are used of the φᾶρος of Calypso, are more applicable to a linen than to a woollen garment. Φᾶρος is the only word used in Homer for the dress of both men and women. When worn by men, the φᾶρος was in all probability draped in the same fashion as the χλαῖνα, but the woman's φᾶρος would be draped differently, as will be shown later.

The χλαῖνα and the φᾶρος were not worn in battle, since they would encumber the wearer too much; armour was put on over the chiton, or in some cases warriors wore the skin of some wild beast slain in combat; we hear, for example, of

---

[1] iii., 126; xxii., 440.   [2] *Odyssey*, ii., 97; xix., 137.
[3] *Ibid.*, v., 257.

Agamemnon wearing a lion's skin,[1] and of Menelaus and Paris wearing leopards' skins.[2]   A man's costume was completed by sandals, πέδιλα, which we are told were made of leather;[3] no mention is made of any head-covering worn in the pursuit of peaceful occupations; if any protection were needed, a fold of the mantle might easily be drawn up over the head; in battle, of course, some kind of helmet was worn, which was made usually of bronze, or sometimes of hide,[4] covered with boars' tusks, such as have been found at Mycenæ.

The women's dress in Homer consists of two garments, the πέπλος and the κρήδεμνον or καλύπτρη, called also in one case the κάλυμμα;[5] the word ἑανός which is used sometimes as a substantive instead of πέπλος, sometimes as an adjective, simply means "something to be worn."

The principal garment of the women was the πέπλος.   The derivation of the word is uncertain; it is probably connected with some root meaning to cover or wrap; the word is used in the *Iliad* to signify things other than dress; for the covering of a chariot[6] and for the wrappings of the vessel which held the ashes of Hector;[7] the πέπλος, therefore, like the χλαῖνα and φᾶρος, consisted of a square or rectangular piece of material which could be used for various purposes.   When worn as a garment, it was held in place by means of brooches

---

[1] *Iliad*, x., 22.   [2] *Ibid.*, 29; iii., 17.   [3] *Odyssey*, xiv., 23.
[4] *Iliad*, x., 261 f.   [5] *Ibid.*, xxiv., 93.
[6] *Ibid.*, v., 194.   [7] *Ibid.*, xxiv., 795.

or pins (περόναι, ἐνεταί) and a girdle. A passage in the *Iliad*[1] gives a description of an elaborate toilette made by Hera when she is setting out to beguile Zeus:

ἀμφὶ δ᾽ ἄρ᾽ ἀμβρόσιον ἑανὸν ἔσαθ᾽ ὃν οἱ Ἀθήνη
ἔξυσ᾽ ἀσκήσασα, τίθει δ᾽ ἐνὶ δαίδαλα πολλά·
χρυσείῃς δ᾽ ἐνετῇσι κατὰ στῆθος περονᾶτο,
ζώσατο δὲ ζώνην ἑκατὸν θυσάνοις ἀραρυῖαν,
ἐν δ᾽ ἄρα ἕρματα ἧκεν εὐτρήτοισι λοβοῖσιν,
τρίγληνα μορόεντα· χάρις δ᾽ ἀπελάμπετο πολλή.
κρηδέμνῳ δ᾽ ἐφύπερθε καλύψατο δῖα θεάων
καλῷ νηγατέῳ, λαμπρὸν δ᾽ ἦν ἠέλιος ὥς.
ποσσὶ δ᾽ ὑπὸ λιπαροῖσιν ἐδήσατο καλὰ πέδιλα.

"Then she clad her in her fragrant robe that Athena wrought delicately for her, and therein set many things beautifully made, and fastened it over her breast with clasps of gold. And she girdled it with a girdle arrayed with a hundred tassels; and she set ear-rings in her pierced ears—ear-rings of three drops and glistering—and therefrom shone grace abundantly. And with a veil over all the peerless goddess veiled herself, a fair, new veil, bright as the sun, and beneath her shining feet she bound goodly sandals."—LANG, LEAF, AND MYERS.

We gather from this passage that the garment was fastened on the shoulders by brooches or pins inserted, κατὰ στῆθος, which Studniczka rightly explains[2] as meaning "down towards the breast," a method of fastening which is represented on the

[1] xiv., 175 f. [2] p. 97 f.

François vase[1] and elsewhere; the material is
drawn from the back, and wraps over that which
covers the front; the pins are then inserted downwards, and hold the two thicknesses of material
together; the dress is held in to the figure by a
girdle worn round the waist, over which any superfluous length of material could be drawn, forming a
κόλπος or pouch.   No mention is made in Homer of
the ἀπόπτυγμα, or overfold, which is a common
feature of the women's dress in historic times ; but
from its constant appearance on the earliest monuments, it is not unreasonable to suppose that it
formed an element in women's costume of the
draped type from the very earliest times.   It is
formed by folding over the upper edge of the
garment before it is put on, in such a way that a
double thickness of material covers the figure from
the neck to a distance a little above the waist in
front and behind.   The original purpose of this
overfold may have been either to secure greater
warmth, or to prevent the dress from tearing at the
points where the brooches were inserted; such a
thing might easily happen, if only the single stuff
were used, since the whole mass of material hung
down from the two points where it was secured on
the shoulders.

Another question which arises in connection
with the Homeric peplos is as to whether it was
worn open or closed at the side; a passage which
has been much discussed in this relation is the one

---

[1] Fig. 8.

which describes the peplos given by Antinous to
Penelope, with its twelve brooches :

Ἀντινόῳ μὲν ἔνεικε μέγαν περικαλλέα πέπλον
ποικίλον· ἐν δ' ἄρ' ἔσαν περόναι δυοκαίδεκα πᾶσαι
χρυσείαι, κληῖσιν εὐγνάμπτοις ἀραρυῖαι.

[*Odyssey*, xviii., 292.]

"For Antinous, his henchman, bare a broidered
robe, great and very fair, wherein were golden
brooches, twelve in all, fitted with well-bent clasps."
—BUTCHER AND LANG.

The point in dispute is the purpose of the
twelve brooches. Studniczka maintains that two
were used to fasten the dress on the shoulders,
and the remaining ten to hold it together down
the open side ; he states in support of this theory
that sewing was not commonly practised by the
Homeric women, although he has previously
pointed out that the men's chiton was always
sewn ; this being the case, it is only natural to
suppose that the women applied the art of sewing
to their own garments also where necessary.
There is no example in early art of a peplos
fastened in this way with brooches ; it is invariably
joined round, the seam being covered by a band of
ornament either woven in the edge of the material
or embroidered upon it afterwards.   In fifth century
art we sometimes find representations of the peplos
worn open down the side ; it may have been worn
so also in Homeric times ; if the garment were
wide, one edge could easily be wrapped over the
other and held in place by the girdle, so as not to

leave the figure too much exposed. It is more
probable that the twelve brooches in question were
used to fasten the dress on the shoulders and down
the upper arms six on each side, forming a kind of
sleeve to the elbow. That the ample Ionic chiton
was worn in this way in later times is manifest from
the numerous vase-paintings and other monuments
of the late sixth and early fifth centuries; it may
have been a fashion peculiar to the East in
Homeric times, but Eastern fashions and customs
were not unknown to the author of the Homeric
poems. We read[1] of rich robes that were the work
of Sidonian women whom Paris brought from
Sidon, and it is not unlikely that Antinous, wishing to offer Penelope some rich gift, would choose
a luxurious garment brought from the East.

However, we must regard the use of twelve
brooches as exceptional, and consider that the
peplos was ordinarily fastened with only two, and
with a girdle round the waist. That it was a fairly
ample garment and trailed on the ground behind, is
proved by the epithets τανυπέπλος and ἑλκεσιπέπλος,
"with trailing robes," frequently applied to women.
Athena finds it certainly too cumbersome to fight
in; for when she is preparing for battle, we are told
that she lets her peplos slip to the ground, and puts
on the chiton of her father,[2] Zeus. A very constant
epithet of the peplos is ποικίλος, or sometimes the
intensified form, παμποίκιλος.[3] The meaning of the

---

[1] *Iliad*, vi., 289.　　　[2] *Ibid.*, v., 733; viii., 385.
[3] *Odyssey*, xv., 105; xviii., 292.

adjective is, "bright, varied, covered with patterns."
Whether these patterns were woven in the material
at the loom or embroidered is a question not easy
to decide.[1]

In some cases they were apparently woven, in
others probably embroidered.

The silver-shining φᾶρος which Calypso puts on [2]
takes the place of the peplos, and was probably worn
in the same way,[3] with the overfold and girdle, over
which the superfluous length was drawn, forming
the κόλπος, or pouch, which varied in depth according to the wearer's fancy. That it was sometimes
fairly roomy is proved by the fact that the nurse of
Eumæus was able to hide three cups ὑπὸ κόλπῳ [4]
"under the folds of her dress."

The material of which the girdle (ζώνη) was made
is uncertain. We hear of golden girdles of Calypso
and Circe, and of a fringed girdle of Hera with a
hundred tassels, but these are exceptional. The
ordinary girdle may have been of metal, or cord, or
leather ; this last material is suggested by the
magic κεστὸς ἱμᾶς of Aphrodite, which may have
been a girdle ; or, since we are told that the goddess
took it ἀπὸ στήθεσφιν,[5] "from her bosom," and that
Hera received it and ἑῷ ἐγκάτθετο κόλπῳ, "put it on
her own bosom," perhaps it was something of the
nature of Athena's ægis, which also possessed magic
power. On a vase in the British Museum [6] a god-

---

[1] See section on "Materials and Ornamentation."
[2] *Odyssey*, v., 230.
[3] The passage is repeated word for word of Circe, *Odyssey*, x., 543.
[4] *Odyssey*, xv., 469.   [5] *Iliad*, xiv., 214.   [6] B., 254.

dess is represented wearing an ægis, and would
naturally be interpreted as Athena, were it not that
the vase-painter has clearly written her name,
"Aphrodite," by her side. It has been suggested
that he has made a slip, and meant to write
"Athena"; but in all probability he knew what he
was doing, and it was his intention to represent
Aphrodite wearing her κεστὸς ἱμάς.

The second garment which was essential to the
completion of a woman's dress, at least when she
appeared in public, was the κρήδεμνον or καλύπτρη,[1]
which served both as cloak and veil. It was probably put on over the shoulders like a shawl, without
being folded, in such a way that it could be drawn
over the head without difficulty, and across the face,
serving as a veil.[2] Sometimes it may have been
doubled corner to corner diagonally and laid on the
shoulder. That it was worn over the head is clear
from *Odyssey*, v., 229, where Calypso puts on her
φᾶρος; κεφαλῇ δ᾽ ἐρύπερθε καλύπτρην, "and over her
head a veil." From the description of Penelope,
when she appears among the suitors "holding her
shining veil before her cheeks," we may gather that
it was customary for women to veil themselves
before men.[3] No woman would think of leaving

---

[1] The κάλυμμα κυάνεον, "dark blue veil," of Thetis (*Iliad*, xxiv., 93) is
the same garment.

[2] Hera is represented wearing it so on the François vase, Fig. 7 (*c*),
and although her head is not covered, yet, from the way in which the
folds lie high upon the nape of the neck, it is clear that they could
easily be drawn up over the head (cp. also, Aphrodite, on the same vase).

[3] Thetis is represented in the François vase just about to veil or
unveil her face; though the head is missing, it is clear, from the
position of the arm, that the κρήδεμνον was worn over the head.

the house without her κρήδεμνον. Helen, though she
quits her house in haste, first veils herself with
shining linen,[1] ἀργεννῇσι καλυψαμένη ὀθόνῃσιν, and it is
only when they are far from the town and enjoying
the quietude of the river bank, that Nausicaa and
her attendant maidens throw off their veils for the
ballplay.[2]

From the constant use of the epithets λιπαρός
and λαμπρός, "shining" or "bright," we may infer
that the κρήδεμνον was usually made of linen, and, in
summer at least, it was probably a fine, light
garment, possibly even semi-transparent. In no
case are any pins or brooches mentioned in connection with it; and from the ease with which it can
be slipped off,[3] it is reasonable to infer that it was
worn without fastening of any kind, like a shawl or
scarf. In the passage where Andromache casts off
her head-dress in her anguish at the death of
Hector,[4] Studniczka supposes that because the
κρήδεμνον is mentioned as falling off last, the other
δέσματα must have been worn over it and held it in
place; this seems to be putting a too literal and
even prosaic interpretation upon the lines. There
is no occasion to suppose that the poet enumerated
the various parts of the head-dress in the order in
which they fell; and if we read in that spirit, we shall
frequently find that the Homeric heroes put on their
cloaks before their undergarments; for more than
once the φᾶρος or χλαῖνα is mentioned before the χιτών.[5]

[1] *Iliad*, iii., 141. [2] *Odyssey*, vi., 100.
[3] Cp. *Iliad*, xxii., 406, 470. [4] *Ibid.*, xxii., 468 f.
[5] *Odyssey*, xvi., 173; xxiii., 155, etc.

The various parts which composed this head-
dress have given rise to much discussion. The
passage runs :

τῆλε δ' ἀπὸ κρατὸς βάλε δέσματα σιγαλόεντα,
ἄμπυκα κεκρύφαλόν τέ ἰδὲ πλεκτὴν ἀναδέσμην
κρήδεμνον θ'.   [*Iliad*, xxii., 468.]

" And far from her head she flung the shining bonds,
diadem and kerchief, and meshy net and veil."

The δέσματα σιγαλόεντα are explained by the
words which follow, and which stand in apposition.
No question is raised as to the nature of the ἄμπυξ ;
it was a metal diadem like the στεφάνη, worn across
the front of the hair. The κρήδεμνον has already been
explained ; the κεκρύφαλος and the πλεκτὴ ἀναδέσμη
need some comment. The former is sometimes
taken to mean a "net," but it will be shown later
that this meaning is better applied to the πλεκτὴ
ἀναδέσμη ; the word κεκρύφαλος is obviously connected
with the verb κρύπτω to cover, and therefore means
"something which covers," "a covering." In all
probability, then, the κεκρύφαλος is simply a kerchief
worn on top of the head behind the ἄμπυξ. The
ἀναδέσμη is obviously something which serves to bind
up (ἀναδέω) the hair and hold it in place, which is
the proper function of a net. The epithet πλεκτή,
which Helbig[1] has tried to explain as "folded,"
means primarily "plaited" ; it is applied elsewhere
in the Homeric poems to baskets,[2] which shows its
perfect appropriateness to the meshes of a net. We

---

[1] *Die Homerische Epos*, p. 157, f.   [2] *Iliad*, xviii., 40.

need give no other meaning, then, to the πλεκτή ἀναδέσμη, but can easily explain it as a net that confined the long hair behind. This completes the head-dress proper, the κρήδεμνον being a separate scarf or shawl worn over it.

The women's dress in Homer is completed by sandals, and for ornament they wore, in addition to the brooches which fastened their clothes, ear-rings and necklaces of varied workmanship; the γναμπταὶ ἕλικες and κάλυκες of which we read [1] are perhaps spiral-shaped brooches and ear-rings or necklaces in the shape of lilies, such as have been found in the later Mycenæan graves.

Few colours are mentioned in Homer in connection with dress. The epithets "white" and "shining" are frequently applied to the chiton and κρήδεμνον and to the φάρος. Φοινικόεις and πορφύρεος are frequently used of the χλαῖνα and the δίπλαξ, the former meaning "red," and the latter probably "dark purple"; the word is used also of the sea and of clouds. The veil of Thetis [2] is described as κυάνεος, indigo, probably, or blue-black, since we hear immediately afterwards that "no garment ever was blacker." The dark veil may be a sign of mourning; but in any case, the epithet might be used of the garments of the sea-goddess, just as κυανοχαίτης, "blue-haired," is applied to Poseidon. Only once is yellow mentioned, and that in the case of "saffron robed dawn." The veil of Hera, that was "bright as the sun," [3] might have

---

[1] *Odyssey*, ix., 247.   [2] *Iliad*, xxiv., 93.   [3] *Iliad*, xiv., 182.

been yellow-gold. Yellow is a favourite colour among the Greek peasant women of to-day for the kerchiefs with which they cover their heads ; and in the clear atmosphere and brilliant sunshine of Greece, it is natural to wear bright colours.

The embroidered robes of the women would naturally be worked in various colours, among which red and blue probably predominated, as they do on the sixth century statues on the Acropolis at Athens, and also in more modern Greek embroideries.

Enough has been said on the subject of Homeric dress to show that it differs entirely from the pre-Hellenic type of costume which appears on the monuments from Knossos and elsewhere. The absence of contemporary monumental evidence renders it impossible to make any very definite statements as to the details of Homeric dress ; but the poems themselves afford sufficient proof of the fact that it was of the draped type, and resembled Greek dress as we know it from the monuments dating from historic times ; the dress of the classical period is simply a development of that described in the Homeric poems, with the addition of some foreign elements which blended with it and some-what transformed it in its details, while still pre-serving the main types unaltered.

III

DORIC

WHEN we come to the question of Greek dress
during the classical period, we find that the literary
evidence is somewhat scanty ; however, in addition
to the various casual references to dress that are to
be found chiefly in the plays, there are a few
passages which bear directly on the historical
development of dress in Greece. The most
important of these is a passage in Herodotus,[1] in
which he describes a disastrous expedition against
Ægina undertaken by the Athenians during the
first half of the sixth century, probably in the year
568 B.C. ; only one man returned alive to Athens, to
meet with an ignominious death at the hands of
the wives of those who had perished. Herodotus
shall tell the story in his own words :

Κομισθεὶς γὰρ ἐς τὰς Ἀθήνας ἀπήγγειλε τὸ πάθος·
πυθομένας δὲ τὰς γυναῖκας τῶν ἐπ᾽ Αἴγιναν στρατευσαμένων
ἀνδρῶν δεινόν τι ποιησαμένας ἐκεῖνον μοῦνον ἐξ ἁπάντων
σωθῆναι, πέριξ τὸν ἄνθρωπον τοῦτον λαβούσας καὶ κεντεύσας
τῇσι περόνῃσι τῶν ἱματίων εἰρωτᾶν ἑκάστην αὐτέων ὅ κῃ εἴη
ὁ ἑωυτῆς ἀνήρ. Καὶ τοῦτον μὲν οὕτω διαφθαρῆναι, Ἀθην-

---

[1] v., 87.

αἴοισι δὲ ἔτι τοῦ πάθεος δεινότερον τι δόξαι εἶναι τὸ τῶν γυναικῶν ἔργον. Ἄλλῳ μὲν δὴ οὐκ ἔχειν ὅτεῳ ζημιώσωσι τὰς γυναῖκας, τὴν δὲ ἐσθῆτα μετέβαλον αὐτέων ἐς τὴν Ἰάδα· ἐφόρεον γὰρ δὴ πρὸ τοῦ αἱ τῶν Ἀθηναίων γυναῖκες ἐσθῆτα Δωρίδα τῇ Κορινθίῃ παραπλησιωτάτην· μετέβαλον ὦν ἐς τὸν λίνεον κιθῶνα, ἵνα δὴ περόνῃσι μὴ χρεώνται. Ἔστι δὲ ἀληθεῖ λόγῳ χρεωμένοισι οὐκ Ἰὰς αὕτη ἡ ἐσθὴς τὸ παλαιὸν, ἀλλὰ Κάειρα, ἐπεὶ ἥ γε Ἑλληνικὴ ἐσθὴς πᾶσα ἡ ἀρχαίη τῶν γυναικῶν ἡ αὐτὴ ἦν τὴν νῦν Δωρίδα καλεῦμεν.

"When he came back to Athens bringing word of the calamity, the wives of those who had been sent out on the expedition took it sorely to heart, that he alone should have survived the slaughter of all the rest; they therefore crowded round the man and struck him with the brooches by which their dresses were fastened, each, as she struck, asking him where he had left her husband. And the man died in this way. The Athenians thought the deed of the women more horrible even than the fate of the troops. As, however, they did not know how else to punish them, they changed their dress, and compelled them to wear the costume of the Ionians. Till this time the Athenian women had worn a Dorian dress, shaped nearly like that which prevails at Corinth. Henceforth they were made to wear the linen tunic, which does not require brooches.

"In very truth, however, this dress is not originally Ionian, but Carian; for anciently the Greek women all wore the costume which is now called the Dorian."—RAWLINSON.

He goes on to say that after this the Argive

and Æginetan women, out of rivalry with the Athenians, wore much larger brooches than before.

The importance of the passage is that it tells us of the two types of dress worn by Greek women. We learn that down to the early years of the sixth century all the Greek women wore the Dorian dress fastened with pins of such size and strength that they could become dangerous weapons in the hands of women excited by grief or passion. Later the Athenian women adopted a different dress, which did not need these large pins to fasten it, and which Herodotus calls the linen Ionic chiton, afterwards correcting himself and explaining that this kind of dress was really Carian in its origin.

The story of the slaying of the sole survivor of the Æginetan expedition, and of the punishment meted out to the Athenian women, seems in itself far-fetched and highly improbable; but there is probably some foundation of truth in it. Possibly the tale was invented by Herodotus, or, more probably, was current in his day as an explanation of a change in the style of dress which actually took place in Athens at the beginning of the sixth century, or more probably even earlier. Among the sumptuary laws introduced by Solon was one regulating women's dress, and forbidding them to wear more than three garments when they went out to funerals or festivals.[1] The passing of such a law could only be necessary if the Athenian women had already adopted a luxurious and

[1] Plutarch, "Solon," 21.

F

extravagant style of dress.   Now, the essence of the
Doric dress, as will be shown later, is simplicity ; it
did not admit of great variety or elaboration.   On
the other hand, that the Ionic dress was somewhat
luxurious is clear from Thucydides, i., 6 ; so we
may infer that by the time of Solon's archonship,
594 B.C., the Athenian women had already adopted
the Ionic dress, and had perhaps elaborated it by
some modifications added by their own invention.
If this is so, Herodotus's story places the change at
least a generation later than its actual occurrence ;
but as he is writing at a distance of more than a
century from the event, we need not be surprised
if he is a generation or so out in his dating.

The simple Doric dress mentioned by Herodotus
as being universally worn by Greek women down
to the sixth century, finds abundant illustration in
early art, especially in the Attic black-figured vases.
It consists of a large oblong piece of material, in
length about 1 ft. more than the height of the
wearer, in width about twice the distance from
elbow to elbow when the wearer's arms are held
out horizontally at shoulder level.   The additional
foot in height is used up by folding the upper edge
over so that the material is double from neck to
waist.   The garment is put on by folding it round
the body and pinning it on the shoulders at points
a third of the distance from the middle line and
the edges respectively.   A diagram will make the
arrangement clear.

a, *b*, *c*, *d* represents the original rectangular

piece of material, *ab* being twice the wearer's
distance from elbow to elbow—that is to say, about
5 ft. 9 in.—*ac* being 1 ft. more than the wearer's
height—namely, about 6 ft. 6 in.

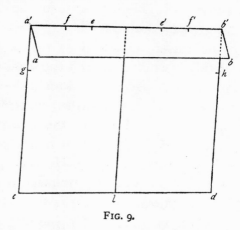

FIG. 9.

After the upper edge *ab* has been folded over to
a width of about 1 ft., the dress is pinned on the
shoulders at the points *e e'* and *f f'*; the part which
covers the back is drawn slightly forward over the
front, so that there are four thicknesses of material
where the pins are inserted; the garment is then
girded at the waist, the position of which is indicated
by the points *g* and *h*, and any superfluous length is
drawn up over the girdle.

The distance between the points *a' f, f e, e' f'*,
etc., varies slightly, but is always approximately
one-sixth of the whole width of the material. In
practice, a better effect is produced if the width of
stuff *e' f'*, which covers the back of the neck, is
shorter than the other sections.

The garment is usually represented as being
sewn up along the side, sometimes along the whole
length *ac*, *bd*, sometimes only along the length
from the waist to the feet—that is, along the edges
gc, *hd*; sometimes it is left open, being held in place
only by the girdle. On the black-figured vases it
is usually the closed Doric dress which is represented, probably because it offered the least difficulty
to a technique which necessarily imposed somewhat
close limitations on the artists who practised it. A
good example is to be found in the figures of the
Fates from the François vase, which has already
been quoted in illustration of the Homeric peplos.

A freer and more realistic representation is to
be found in the sculptured metopes from the temple
of Zeus, at Olympia. Athena in the metope representing the cleaning of the Augean stables wears
the closed Doric dress; here the ἀπόπτυγμα, or
overfold, falls slightly below the waist, and below
it the kolpos is clearly visible, the slight pouch
formed by drawing the superfluous length of the
material over the girdle.[1] On the vases the pouch
is almost invariably absent, and the girdle is always
visible. This is also the case in one of the archaic
statues on the Acropolis at Athens, where the Doric
dress is worn over an Ionic chiton. A slight varia-
tion of the dress is to be seen on the nymph of the
Atlas metope at Olympia, where the overfold hangs
considerably below the waist and no girdle or pouch
is visible; here the additional length of the overfold

[1] Fig. 10.

probably obviated the necessity of a pouch, and the girdle, which is hidden, simply served to hold the dress in to the figure. A bronze statuette from Herculaneum shows the dress sewn up only from the waist downwards (Fig. 11).

As time went on, the dimensions of the Doric dress became more ample, or at least were represented so in art; both pouch and overfold become deeper and the folds of the garment generally grow fuller; the distance of the shoulder pins from the points which hang immediately under the arms becomes proportionately larger, no longer being an exact sixth of the whole width of the dress. The most perfect examples in art of the Doric dress in its full development are to be found in the maidens of the Parthenon frieze and the Caryatids of the Erechtheum. Here the pouch is emphasized, and its graceful curve dipping over the hips, though idealized, is at the same time perfectly naturalistic, as can be shown at once by practical experiment.

The Munich copy of Cephisodotus's Eirene holding the infant Plutus presents a very good example of the closed Doric dress as it was worn in the fourth century; it will be seen that the folds are more ample, and the overfold and pouch fall to a distance considerably below the waist, so that the garment must be larger than that originally worn, if we are to accept early monuments as faithful representations of the style of dress actually worn.

The simpler form of the Doric dress, namely, that which is unsewn and left open down the side, is not found represented in art before the fifth century ; it becomes fairly common on red-figured vases, where it is very frequently depicted ungirt.[1] Sometimes it is the only garment worn ; in other cases it is worn over an under-dress. A sculptured example is to be found in an Artemis in Dresden,[2] for the original of which Fürtwängler claims Praxitelean authorship. This was probably the dress worn by Laconian girls, to whom the term φαινομηρίς, "showing the thigh," was applied by some ancient writers.[3]

A variety of this dress appears in art about the middle of the fifth century ; it is sometimes known as the "peplos of Athena," because Pheidias chose it as the style in which to drape his statue of the Athena Parthenos. The word "peplos" is usually reserved for the Doric dress whether open or closed, the word "chiton" for the Ionic, though the latter is frequently applied to the Doric, and is invariably used of the under-dress, when the two styles became confused. The "peplos of Athena" is similar to the ordinary open Doric dress, except that the over-fold is longer and reaches to the thighs and the girdle is worn over it.[4] The material is pulled up very slightly over the girdle, but not sufficiently to hide it in front, the purpose of the slight pouch being merely to prevent the dress from dragging under the arms, and from trailing on the ground at the sides. The girdle is at first worn round the

---

[1] Fig. 12. [2] Fürtwängler, *Masterpieces*, p. 324.
[3] Pollux, II., 187. [4] Fig. 13.

waist, but later it is put on higher, until, on the Athena from the frieze of the altar at Pergamon, it is worn immediately under the breasts. The clearest representation in art is to be found in the Varvakeion copy of the Athena Parthenos, and it occurs also in many representations of Athena which were obviously influenced by Pheidias. In the Dresden "Lemnia,"[1] the girdle is passed not only over the overfold, but also round the ægis; in the "torso Medici"[2] this overgirt peplos is worn over an under-dress of the Ionic type. The date of the introduction of this style of wearing the Doric dress is a point of some uncertainty. The question arises as to whether it was invented by Pheidias or was already commonly worn and adopted by him as being most appropriate for his great representation of the maiden goddess. Certainly, in sculpture we have no example of it before the time of Pheidias, unless we assign an earlier date to the little relief of the "mourning Athena," which seems improbable; the Iris of the Parthenon frieze wears it; and among slightly later works the Victory of Pæonius at Olympia is a good example, though here the dress is slightly varied by being fastened only on one shoulder. Further evidence is afforded by the vases, but even these do not give any certain proof; the dress does not appear before the middle of the fifth century, but after that date it becomes fairly frequent, and is given not only to Athena but to other divine or mythological personages, such as

[1] Fürtwängler, pl. ii.   [2] *Ibid.*, fig. 6.

Persephone,[1] Nike, Cassandra, and also to hand-maids attending on ladies in more elaborate costume. In some of these vases the work is obviously post-Pheidian, but many of them were probably made before the completion of the Athena Parthenos, and the fact that the overgirt dress is so frequently represented on slaves renders it likely that it was a style of dress actually worn, and not merely the invention of the great sculptor's imagination; it was probably selected by him for the Parthenos because of its extreme simplicity and the possibilities of statuesque dignity which it contained.

It has been mentioned incidentally that the Doric peplos is sometimes found worn over another garment, but it is ordinarily the only garment worn indoors, and for outdoor wear another is sometimes put on over it. The overfold of the peplos could itself be used as a veil by drawing the back part up over the head; it is so used by a woman on a red-figured vase in the British Museum.[2]

The outer garment worn by women in classical times corresponds to the Homeric κρήδεμνον and is called the ἱμάτιον, although this term is applied by Herodotus to the Doric peplos. By derivation the word simply means "a piece of clothing," being connected with εἷμα and ἕννυμι. It consisted of a large oblong piece of material about 7 or 8 feet in length, and in breadth about equal to the wearer's height. Considerable variety was possible

[1] B.M., E. 183. [2] E. 307.

in the arrangement of it. It could be worn both as head covering and cloak, by placing the middle of the upper edge over the head and letting the two sides fall down over the shoulders like a shawl; it is often so depicted on the vases both black- and red-figured; the figure of Eleusis wears it so on the Triptolemus vase by Hieron in the British Museum.[1] It was frequently worn over the shoulders in this fashion without covering the head, and could easily be pushed back or drawn up over the head at will. A second very common way of arranging the himation was to draw one end over the left shoulder from the back towards the front, so that it hung down in a point in front, then to pass the mass of material across the back and under the right arm and throw the other end over the left shoulder again, so that the second point hung down towards the back: this was a very common style both for men and women.[2] If additional warmth were required, it could easily be obtained by drawing the cloak up over the right shoulder, so as not to leave the right arm and chest exposed. A combination of these two styles is seen in some of the Tanagra statuettes, where the himation is put on over the head. Both shoulders are covered; but instead of the two ends being allowed to hang down symmetrically one on each side of the front, one is taken up and thrown over the other shoulder, so that the whole figure is covered in the ample folds of the cloak.[3]

[1] Fig. 14, the figure to the right in the upper band.
[2] See Fig. 20.   [3] Fig. 15.

A rather exceptional variant of the second style
of wearing the himation is to be seen on a vase of
Euxitheos in the British Museum,[1] where Briseis is
represented wearing it with one end placed on the
left shoulder, the mass of the cloak being drawn
across the back ; the other end is passed under the
right arm, but instead of being thrown over the left
shoulder again, is turned back over the right
shoulder, and so leaves the front of the figure
exposed.

A third fashion is somewhat similar to the
second, except that it leaves the front of the figure
exposed to the waist or a little below. Instead of
being drawn across the chest and thrown over the
left shoulder, the second end is simply thrown over
the forearm and held in place by the bend of the
elbow.[2] A cloak worn in this style would be very
likely to slip, so another fashion was adopted, which
produced approximately the same effect, but which
prevented the possibility of slipping. Instead of
throwing the end over the left arm, the wearer
secured it at the waist under the arm either by a
brooch or more probably by simply tucking it under
the girdle. To prevent the garment from hanging
down too low and dragging on the ground, a large
corner was usually doubled over before it was
secured at the waist. The part thus fastened was
sometimes passed over the end which hung down
from the left shoulder, sometimes under it. The
himation is so worn by Mausolus and Artemisia in

[1] E. 258, fig. 16.   [2] Fig. 17.

their portrait statues from the Mausoleum. A very good example is the Athena of Velletri published by Fürtwängler.[1]

On many of the monuments of the Pheidian period and the time immediately preceding it, we find that the Doric peplos is worn alone or with a small cloak or shawl laid on the shoulders and hanging down the back, as in the case of the maidens carrying sacrificial vessels on the Parthenon frieze. This small shawl was perhaps worn more for ornament than for the sake of warmth, and an ample peplos of warm woollen material might be found sufficient protection.

It may be objected that in the majority of the examples chosen as illustrations the himation is worn not over the Doric peplos, but over the Ionic chiton, and it has indeed been sometimes regarded as an element of the Ionic dress rather than of the Doric.

It does, however, appear over the Doric peplos, e.g., in Fig. 18 and on many black-figured Attic vases,[2] and it is not difficult to trace its development from the Homeric κρήδεμνον worn symmetrically over the head and shoulders. It is an easy step in advance to throw one end of the cloak over the opposite shoulder, push it back off the head, and bring one arm out free instead of letting it remain covered. Fig. 15 might serve to illustrate an inter-mediate stage between those represented in Figs. 14 and 17.

An attempt will be made later to show that the

[1] *Masterpieces*, p. 142, fig. 18.   [2] B.M., B. 331.

Ionic himation was fastened with brooches, and had a different development. The wearing of the un-pinned himation over the Ionic chiton is an instance of the blending of Doric and Ionic dress.

The Doric dress of men was similar to that of women, both with regard to under-dress and cloak. The name χιτών is used for the under-dress, as it was in Homer, the word peplos being restricted to women's garments. The outer garment of men as well as of women is called the himation.

The Doric men's chiton is fastened by brooches on the shoulders and girt in at the waist. It was a short garment reaching midway down the thighs, or to a distance just above the knees, had no over-fold, and was narrower than the women's peplos. No kolpos was worn, there being no superfluous length to dispose of. The side was sewn up so that the garment before being pinned was cylindrical in shape. This somewhat scanty garment was the only one worn by slaves, and men engaged in active pursuits and workmen frequently wore it fastened only on one shoulder, leaving the other bare and the arm quite free. When worn in this way it was called the χιτών ἔξωμις or ἑτερομάσχαλος; the god Hephaistos is usually represented wearing it in this way in his capacity as craftsman. We learn from Pollux, vii., 47, that the ἔξωμις was a περιβλῆμα as well as an ἔνδυμα, from which we may gather that a small cloak was sometimes worn fastened on one shoulder and girt round the waist, but left unsewn down the side. Fig. 19 represents the χιτών ἔξωμις.

Representations of Amazons and of Artemis the huntress are frequent, wearing the χιτὼν ἔξωμις; but in these cases it is usually a longer garment than that worn by men, and its superfluous length is drawn up over the girdle, forming a pouch; and then a second girdle is worn over this to prevent it from flapping in the wind. The Amazons of the Mausoleum frieze wear the short Doric dress without overfold and unsewn down the side; this, however, is perhaps merely a device on the part of the sculptor to afford an opportunity of displaying the physical forms, as well as the drapery. Various references in literature show that the Spartan women wore more scanty clothing than the Athenians; they are described as μονοχίτων, "wearing a single garment," and we learn from Pausanias that the girls who competed in the running races at Olympia wore the short χιτὼν ἔξωμις. As monumental testimony to the truth of this statement, we have the statue of a girl runner in the Vatican Museum.

The τρίβων worn by Spartans and people of austere or Laconizing tendencies, like Socrates and the Cynic philosophers, was probably a scanty Doric chiton made in some coarse homespun material; men of leisure and elderly men preferred to wear a longer chiton with sleeves either sewn or fastened with brooches; this was the case even after the reaction against anything savouring of Orientalism which followed the Persian wars. If we are to consider the monuments, both sculpture and vases, as giving a realistic picture of Greek life, we shall see that men frequently wore only the himation ; but it is difficult to believe that this was so, except, perhaps, in the height of summer.

The methods of draping the himation were the same for men as for women, except that after the period of the early black-figured vases we do not find men represented wearing it laid on both shoulders like a shawl ; nor do they ever wear it drawn up over the head, although in the sunshine of a southern summer some such protection against the heat might be considered indispensable. The favourite style for men was that of laying the one end on the left shoulder and drawing the rest round the body from the back and throwing the other end either across the left forearm or over the shoulder.[1] This was called wearing the himation ἐπὶ δεξιὰ, presumably because it was drawn closely round the right side of the body. It was considered a mark of good breeding to throw it over the shoulder and let it hang down in such a way as to cover the left arm completely.[2] To wear it ἐπ᾽ ἀριστέρα, "over the left side," was a mark of boorishness, as we gather from Aristophane's *Birds*,[3] where Poseidon taunts the barbarian Triballus for wearing it so.

Another variety of over-garment worn by men is the χλάμυς, a cloak used for riding or travelling. It is considered to be of Macedonian origin,[4] another form of it being the ζειρά, a rough Thracian riding-

---

[1] Figs. 20 and 21.   [2] Fig. 20.   [3] i., 1567.
[4] Pauly-Wissowa, *Real Encyclopädie.*

FIG. 2O.—Vase-painting—British Museum.

FIG. 21.—The Doric Himation.

FIG. 22.—Vase-painting by Euphronios—Munich.
[Fürtwängler and Reichhold, *Griechische Vasenmalerei*, 22.]

Fig. i. Detail from an Attic kylix (ca. 440 B.C.), British Museum.

FIG. 23.—The Chlamys and Petasos.

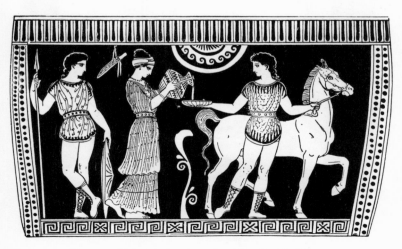

FIG. 25.—Vase-painting from Lucania—British Museum.

FIG. 28.—Vase-painting—Munich.
[Fürtwängler and Reichhold, *Griechische Vasenmalerei*, 33.]

cloak sometimes depicted on Greek vases.[1] It was probably brought into Greece from the north by the Dorian invaders when they came down, and in its origin may have been no different from the Homeric χλαῖνα. In classical times it was always worn over the short chiton by travellers and riders, and was the characteristic dress of Ephebi.[2] The Parthenon frieze affords abundant illustration of the

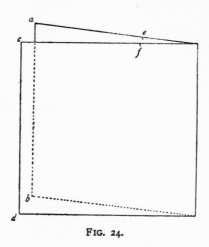

FIG. 24.

way in which it was worn. Like the himation, it consisted of a rectangular piece of material, but was of a slightly different shape, being rather more oblong; in fact, when doubled it would form almost a perfect square. Its normal dimensions would be about 6 to 7 feet long by 3½ feet wide. In putting it on, the wearer would double it round him and stand inside it, so that the middle line came along the back of the left arm and shoulder; he would

[1] Fig. 22.   [2] Fig. 23.

then fasten the two sides together with a brooch on the right shoulder, close to the neck, at the points *e* and *f* in the accompanying diagram ; the corners *d* and *b* would hang down in front and behind respectively at a distance of about 1 foot from the ground, and the corners *a* and *c* would hang down together along the right side ; the left arm which held the reins in riding would thus be covered, while the right would be free to hold spear or whip. The left could easily be freed also by swinging the cloak round so that the brooch came under the chin instead of on the shoulder ; the two corners *a* and *c* could then be thrown back over the arms. The χλάμυς is frequently represented in art worn in this way, especially in cases where the wearer is occupied in vigorous action.

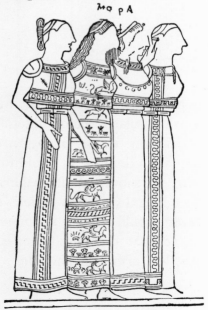

Fig. 8.—From the François Vase.

IV

IONIC

WE must now turn to a consideration of the Ionic dress, which Herodotus tells us was adopted by the Athenian women in the sixth century B.C. According to his account, it was Carian in its origin ; our knowledge of the Carians is somewhat vague and indefinite. We learn from Thucydides[1] that they originally inhabited the Cyclades, but were driven out by Minos of Crete ; and a little later on[2] he speaks of them, together with the Phœnicians, as islanders who practised piracy. Herodotus[3] gives a slightly different account, saying that the Carian inhabitants of the islands were subjected by Minos and used by him to man his ships, and were not driven out until later by the Dorian and Ionian immigrants. He also mentions the belief of the Carians themselves that they were autochthonous in Caria, and attributes to them various inventions afterwards adopted by the Greeks. According to Thucydides, their method of burying the dead seems to have differed from that of the Greeks ; and from the various accounts of the two historians,

[1] i., 4.   [2] i., 8.   [3] i., 171.

we may gather that their race was different, although possibly they were soon hellenized by their Ionian neighbours. If, as Herodotus tells us, the Greeks adopted some Carian inventions, it is not unlikely that they may also have adopted the Carian dress, or at least may have modified their own by assuming some Carian elements.[1]

In his account of the assumption of the Ionic dress by the Athenians, Herodotus speaks only of the women ; but we know that it was worn by men also, partly from the evidence of the monuments and partly from Thucydides, who tells us [2] that not long previously to the time at which he is writing the elder men of the wealthy classes gave up wearing linen chitons and fastening their hair with the τέττιξ, "cicala," a luxurious mode of dress common to them and their kinsfolk the Ionians. The Ionic dress was probably discarded by the Athenians shortly after the outbreak of the Persian war, when a reaction set in against Orientalism and a tendency towards greater simplicity began to manifest itself; Thucydides is writing more than a generation after the Persian wars, but his expression, οὐ πολὺς χρόνος, "no great length of time," is sufficiently vague, and he probably recollected the change which took place in his youthful days ; moreover, he speaks only of the elder men of the wealthy classes, who would naturally be of conserva-

---

[1] According to Ridgeway, *Early Age of Greece*, the Carians, like the Leleges, were a Pelasgian people.
[2] i., 6.

tive tendencies and the last to adopt any change in
their mode of life or dress.   The exact period at
which the Athenians adopted the Ionic dress is
unknown ; the Æginetan expedition of 568 B.C., of
which Herodotus makes use in dating the change,
is too late, for we know that already in Solon's days
luxury in dress had reached such a pitch as to
necessitate the passing of a sumptuary law to
regulate it, and such luxury could hardly have been
reached so long as the simple Doric dress was
retained.   It may not be unreasonable to assume,
then, that constant intercourse with the Ionians in
the islands on the coast of Asia Minor led the
Athenians to adopt their dress at some time
towards the end of the seventh century.

The Ionic chiton differed from the Doric in
length, material, and method of fastening.   We read
in Homer already of the Ἰάωνες ἑλκεχίτωνες, "long-
robed Ionians," and Pollux tells us of the λινοῦς χιτών
ὃν Ἀθηναῖοι ἐφόρουν ποδήρη, καὶ αὖθις Ἴωνες,[1] "the linen
tunic which the Athenians wore reaching to the
feet, and the Ionians too."   This χιτὼν ποδήρης is a
long chiton reaching to the feet ; that its material
was linen is testified by Thucydides and Pollux, as
well as other writers.[2]   The story of Herodotus
shows that its fastening was different from that of
the Doric, since the Athenian women were forced
to adopt it, ἵνα δὴ περόνῃσι μὴ χρεώνται, "so as not to

---

[1] *Poll.*, vii., 49.
[2] Studniczka has pointed out that the word χιτών is of Semitic
origin, and connected with a root signifying "linen," *Beiträge*, p. 17 f.

need brooches." This expression is usually taken
to mean that the characteristic difference between
the Doric and Ionic chitons is, that the Doric is
fastened by means of pins or brooches, the Ionic is
always sewn on the shoulders. That this is not
invariably the case is proved by many examples
both in sculpture and vase-painting, where a chiton
is represented, which, from its length and fulness
and the fine texture of its material, is clearly Ionic,
but which is not sewn on the shoulders, but fastened
together down the upper arm by a series of small
round brooches; this fastening forms a kind of
loose sleeve which reaches frequently to the elbow.
It is the formation of this sleeve, whether sewn or
pinned, which, apart from size or material, distinguishes the Ionic from the Doric chiton, which is
sleeveless. The Ionic chiton in its simplest form is
cylindrical in shape, and varies considerably in
length, but is always longer than the height of the
wearer; the superfluous length is drawn up through
the girdle to form a kolpos, which varies in depth
according to the length of the chiton. The Mænad
vase of Hieron gives a good idea of the size to
which this kolpos sometimes attained.[1] Being
made of a fine linen material, the Ionic chiton is
naturally fuller than the coarser woollen Doric
garment, and its folds are consequently more
numerous and more delicate; it is the greater width
of the garment which necessitates the formation of
the sleeve, as a single fastening from the shoulder

[1] Cp. Fig. 14, the second figure to the right in the lower band.

would leave too great a mass of material hanging
down under the arms.   The sleeve is made by join-
ing the two top edges of the garment together and
gathering them up so as to form regular folds ; an
opening is left in the middle for the neck and one at
each end for the arms.   The arm-holes were probably not formed, as some believe, by lateral openings
in the side-seams, since this method produces a
clumsy effect in practice ; and moreover, in many
vase-paintings[1] the ornamental border which runs
along the neck and upper arm passes also round the
arms without being con-
tinued down the side, which
shows that it was em-
broidered or woven along
the top edge of the chiton
before the sleeves were made.
A diagram will best show
how the sleeves were formed,
and the position of the openings for neck and arms : *ab*
represents the upper edge of
the chiton, along which a

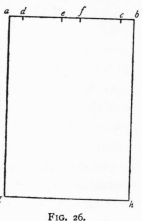

FIG. 26.

border is frequently woven or embroidered ; *ef*
represents the space for the neck, through which
the head is thrust ; *ad* and *bc* represent the
arm-holes, which hang down parallel to the
wearer's sides when the arms are held down in a
normal position ; the side-seams *ag* and *bh* are sewn
along their whole length ; the distances *de fc* are

[1] *E.g.*, B.M., E. 73 ; cp. Fig. 25, the two male figures.

joined and gathered to form the full sleeve. The
fulness is frequently held close to the figure by the
addition of cross-bands, either crossing both in
front and behind and attached to the girdle at the
sides, or crossing only at the back and passing
round the front of the shoulders. A very excellent
sculptured representation of this, the simplest form
of the Ionic chiton, is to be found in the famous
Delphi charioteer, where the gathering of the
sleeves is very clearly marked.[1] In cases where
the sleeve is not sewn, the spaces *de* and *fc* are joined
by a series of brooches, varying in number from four
to six on each side. The fulness is produced by
taking up a little group of folds at each fastening
and leaving the spaces between quite plain ; the two
edges are usually parted in these spaces, so as to
show the arm through. These groups of folds are
perhaps more effective than the continuous row of
gathers which we get with the sewn sleeve. The
Euxitheos vase reproduced above[2] will furnish an
illustration of the chiton with pinned sleeves. A
short chiton, with sleeves pinned in several places,
was frequently worn by men, as is proved by many
vase-paintings. We sometimes find women represented wearing a full chiton without overfold,
fastened only once on each shoulder, like the Doric
dress. This is one of the many modifications which
the Ionic dress underwent when introduced into the
mainland of Greece. We frequently find on vases
figures in rapid motion wearing the long Ionic

[1] Fig. 27.   [2] Fig. 16.

chiton with many folds, represented by fine close lines, in which the lower edge of the chiton in front is drawn up to an angle on one or often more places. It was supposed by Böhlau[1] that this was meant to indicate that the garment had been cut at the bottom in a series of points. The object of this cutting is difficult to see, and on examination it will be found that wherever the lower edge of the chiton is so drawn up, immediately above it the kolpos hangs down deeper over the girdle; the figures are usually in rapid motion, and the lower edge of the back of the garment, which shows behind the feet, is represented by a continuous curve, without being drawn up anywhere.[2] It is obvious, then, that the artist intended to indicate that the wearer had drawn the dress up through the girdle, so as not to impede progress. Anyone who has ever moved about freely wearing a chiton of this kind, will know that unless the girdle is uncomfortably tight the dress has a habit of slipping down, so that it is necessary to pull it up sometimes, so as to prevent treading on it in front.

A feature of the Ionic chiton not very easy to understand is the overfold, which occurs very frequently, especially in vase-paintings of the severe red-figured class; it is not a normal feature of the Ionic chiton, and may very possibly have been added by the Athenian women when they adopted the dress, since they had always been accustomed to wearing it with the Doric peplos. The view

[1] *Quæstiones vestiariæ.*   [2] Fig. 28.

that Herodotus (v., 87) is wrong, and that the
Athenian women never wore the Doric dress at all,
is hardly tenable in the face of such evidence as the
François vase and others like it, which are certainly
of Attic workmanship.

The Ionic chiton with overfold is really, then, an
instance of the blending of the two types of dress,
which later became so complete that it is frequently
difficult to decide whether a particular garment
should more correctly be called Doric or Ionic.

In some instances the overfold of the Ionic
chiton is formed in exactly the same way as that of
the Doric dress, only it is frequently shorter: it is
turned over before the garment is put on, then back
and front are fastened together along the arm, either
by sewing or by brooches. In this latter case the
only distinction from the Doric dress, in addition to
those of size and material, is that instead of being
pinned only once on each shoulder, and so being
sleeveless, it is pinned along from shoulder to elbow,
so as to form sleeves. An example of this is to be
seen in a figure of Aphrodite from a vase-painting
in Paris reproduced by Miss Harrison.[1] This style
of dress, with the sleeves sewn instead of pinned, is
found on the first of the so-called Fates of the
Parthenon pediment, and on one of the Nereids
from the Nereid monument, on a torso at Epidaurus,
and on many vase-paintings. Although not always
represented in art, shoulder-cords or cross-bands
were probably actually worn with this dress, as a

[1] *Prolegomena to Greek Religion*, p. 292.

general rule, since without some such contrivance it would slip inconveniently.

A type of dress very commonly found on vases is that which has full sleeves to the elbow and an overfold covering the chest and back, and passing under the arms without covering the sleeves, as was the case in the chiton described above. The Mænads on the famous Hieron vase are represented wearing this kind of dress, and numerous examples could be quoted from other vase-paintings.[1] Some such effect might be produced with the ordinary cylindrical-shaped chiton with overfold, if shoulder-bands were worn such as those worn by the Delphi Charioteer and by one of the so-called Fates of the east pediment of the Parthenon; but in actual practice such an arrangement would produce a somewhat clumsy mass of folds under the arm, and could not be managed at all unless the overfold were considerably deeper than that usually represented on the vases. We must look, therefore, for some other explanation; and it will not be far to seek, if we allow the Ionian women and their Athenian imitators a freer use of scissors and needle than their Doric sisters were accustomed to make. A close examination of the monuments will show that although the sleeve of the Ionic chiton was frequently formed in the manner described above, yet in a very large number of cases, in almost all of which the overfold is present, the sleeve is more like our modern notion of a sleeve—

[1] Cp. Fig. 29.

I

that is to say, it fits closer to the arm, as though shaped to some extent, while the rest of the garment fits closer to the figure. The vase-painter Brygos is fond of depicting women in this kind of dress : the accompanying illustration [1] is taken from his representation of Hera and Iris pursued by Silenoi. This dress is obviously not composed simply of a cylindrical piece of material

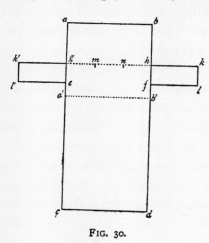

FIG. 30.

folded over at the top and fastened on the arms, for the rather deep overfold leaves the sleeves quite free, and covers only the body of the wearer. This effect could be produced in two ways, in both of which, however, the sleeve-pieces must be sewn in separately. In the first method, we may suppose that two rectangular pieces of material are taken, equal in size and shape, represented in the diagram as *abcd*.

These are sewn together along the sides up to the points *e* and *f*, at a distance of about 5 feet from the lower edge; when the dress is worn, these points will come immediately under the arms. We may next suppose that two rectangular pieces of material measuring about 18 by 20 inches are taken

[1] Fig. 29.

for the sleeves ; these are folded double, so that the
longer sides lie upon each other, and then sewn on
to the body of the chiton at the points f, h, g, and e,
so that the fold lies in the position indicated by the
lines fl and el' in the diagram ; the openings kl and
$k'l'$ will form the arm-holes ; that part of the chiton
$abgh$ which still extends above the sleeve-pieces is
then folded over, so that it hangs down in the
position $gha'b'$. The line kk' now represents the
upper edges of the garment, which are fastened
together (leaving the space mn for the neck) either
by sewing and gathering or by groups of folds held
in place by a series of brooches. The front and
back part of the overfold would then hang down
separately, but they could be joined together under
the arms, provided that the space round the shoulder
were left free for the arm to pass through into the
sleeve.

The second method of making this dress is
nothing but a modification of the first. It consists
of taking two smaller rectangles in the first place,
$ghcd$, to form the body of the chiton ; two pieces
$abgh$ are sewn on back and front, after the sleeve-
pieces, to form a sort of false overfold, which will
have exactly the same effect as if it were in one
piece with the rest of the chiton.

It is possible to conceive of the sleeve-pieces
being originally in one piece with the rest of the
chiton, which would then be a dress composed of
two cross-shaped pieces of material sewn together
along the edges dfl and cel' ; it is more reasonable

to suppose, however, that the sleeve-pieces were sewn on separately. That such sleeve-pieces were attached to the ordinary Ionic chiton without over-fold seems likely from many vase-paintings. The addition of sleeves was certainly not unfamiliar to the Greeks, for we find slaves wearing a narrow, ungirt chiton, with tight sleeves reaching to the wrists. A familiar example of this is to be found in Hegeso's attendant on the well-known grave relief in Athens. In an inscription, dating from the middle of the fourth century,[1] and recording a large number of garments dedicated to Artemis Brauronia, the expression χειριδωτός occurs, which can only mean "sleeved." In the same inscription special mention is frequently made of the fact that the chiton, or χιτωνίσκος, is ἐμπλαισίῳ, "oblong," from which we may infer that it was not always so. Now, the ordinary simple Ionic chiton would be oblong in shape when not worn, so that we may take the others, which are not described as oblong, to be chitons with separate sleeve-pieces attached.

The false overfold was sometimes attached also to the simple cylindrical Ionic chiton. In these cases it covered the chest only, leaving the arms covered only by the sleeves ; it was probably simply sewn on at the neck in front only. Kalkmann has collected and stated the evidence for this false overfold to the chiton in an article in the *Jahrbuch*, vol. xi., where he shows that it was sometimes applied to

[1] *C. I. A.*, ii., 754.

the over-garment also. Very clear examples of it are to be seen in some of the archaic female statues on the Acropolis at Athens, especially in those cases where the himation is worn like a shawl over both shoulders.[1]

That the long Ionic chiton with sleeves was worn by men as well as women, is abundantly evident from the monuments. On the vases, Zeus and Dionysus and other gods are almost invariably represented wearing it; and in sculpture also, kings, priests, and others are represented so dressed. Together with the himation, it probably constituted a sort of state dress for priests and other officials, even after it had been discarded for daily use, as being too luxurious.

A short chiton, with or without sleeves, and made of some fine material, is to be found on the vases worn by men engaged in active pursuits. It sometimes has an overfold; although, with the long chiton, this feature is usually confined to women. A good example of the men's short chiton with overfold is to be seen on the vase of Brygos representing the exploits of Theseus.

The cross-bands and shoulder-cords already mentioned are, strictly speaking, an element of the Ionic chiton, though they are sometimes represented in art over the Doric peplos. Their object is to hold the ample folds of the full chiton close to the figure, and to prevent the sleeves from slipping or flapping about with every movement of the wearer. The

[1] Nos. 687 and 688.

cross-bands are usually attached to the girdle and can be of one piece with it ; their place is sometimes taken by a second girdle, worn rather high over the kolpos, as is the case with the Artemis of Gabii reproduced below (Fig. 37).

This high girdle was known as the ταινία, or ἀποδέσμος, whereas the low girdle was called περιζῶμα. A broad band, known as the στρόφιον, was sometimes worn by women under the breasts, to serve the purpose of modern corsets.[1]

A word or two must be said about the diminutives of χιτών—namely, χιτώνιον, χιτωνάριον, and χιτωνίσκος. We should naturally expect the words to mean a small or short chiton, but this does not seem always to be the case. The χιτώνιον and χιτωνάριον are frequently described as διαφανές, "transparent,"[2] and Eustathius (iii., 1166) explains the words as referring to a fine and luxurious dress worn by women. In the inscription to Artemis Brauronia[3] we read more than once of a χιτώνιον ἀμοργῖνον—that is, a garment made of linen from Amorgos, which we know was very fine and expensive ; we may infer, then, that the diminutives χιτώνιον and χιτωνάριον refer to fineness of material rather than to shortness of cut. The case of the χιτωνίσκος is somewhat different ; it is not referred to as being transparent, and is usually described in the inscription cited above as being very ornate. Women are frequently repre-

---

[1] B.M., Vase, E. 230.
[2] *Ar. Lys.*, 48 ; *Menander Meineke. frag. incert.*, 141.
[3] *C. I. A.*, ii., 754.

sented on vases[1] wearing over the long Ionic
chiton a short and sometimes very ornate garment,
which cannot be described as a himation. Possibly
this short over-chiton is the garment indicated by
the name χιτώνισκος.[2] A similar garment was worn
by musicians over the long ungirt chiton (ὀρθοστάδιος).[3]
Another instance of a special dress worn for a
special purpose is the costume worn by actors ; it
had long sleeves, and was probably padded to complete the impression of increased size produced by
the high masks and buskins.

The himation worn over the Ionic chiton
presents considerable variety of shape and arrangement. In very many cases we find that the Doric
himation is worn, whether over both shoulders or
only over one. In the Harpy monument, where
we might have looked for Ionic dress in its purest
form, we find the Doric himation worn over the
fine linen-sleeved chiton, and on very many of the
red-figured vases of the severe style this is the case.
There is one set of monuments, however, which
may be considered as Ionic in origin, or at least of
Ionizing tendencies, where a far less simple garment
takes the place of the Doric himation. This set
includes the archaic female statues and flying
victories of the Acropolis Museum at Athens, and
a large number of small painted terra-cotta statuettes

[1] *Jahrbuch*, i., pl. 102*a* ; Gerhard, *Anserlesene Vasenbilder*, 79, 80 ;
Dumont and Chaplain, pl. 8 ; *Journal of Hellenic Studies*, 1890, pl. 12.
[2] Cp. Amelung in Pauly-Wissowa's *Real Encyclopädie*, *s.v.*
"Chiton," p. 2322.
[3] B.M., E. 270.

in the same museum, the sculptures of the Treasury of the Cnidians at Delphi, and a number of other statues and reliefs from Athens, Eleusis, Delos, and elsewhere. The dress presents a somewhat complicated appearance at first sight, and has given rise to a considerable amount of discussion. The following section is based upon a careful study of the original monuments and of the literature already written on the subject.

FIG. 17.—Vase-painting by Falerii—Rome, Villa Giulia.

[Fürtwängler and Reichhold, *Griechische Vasenmalerei*, 17 and 18.]

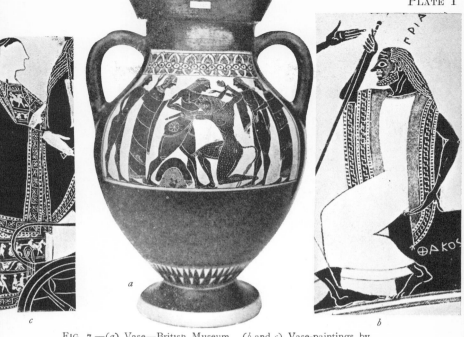

PLATE I

FIG. 7.—(a) Vase—British Museum. (b and c) Vase-paintings by
Klitias and Ergotimos, Florence.
[Fürtwängler and Reichhold, *Griechische Vasenmalerei*, 1 and 11.]

FIG. 29.—Vase-painting by Brygos—British Museum.

FIG. 10.—Metope from the Temple of Zeus, at Olympia.

FIG. 11.—Bronze Statue from Herculaneum, Naples. FIG. 37.—The Artemis of Gabii—Louvre.

PLATE L

FIG. 12.—Vase-painting—British Museum.

FIG. 14.—Vase-painting by Hieron—British Museum.

FIG. 13.—Vase-painting in the Polygnotan Style—Louvre

FIG. 15.—Terra-cotta Statuette—British Museum.

FIG. 16.—Vase-painting by Euxitheos—British M

FIG. 18.—Athena of Velletri.

FIG. 19.—Bronze Statuette—British Museum.

FIG. 27.—The Delphi Charioteer.

FIG. 31.—Archaic Statue—Athens, Acropolis Museum.

FIG. 32.—Archaic Statue—Athens, Acropolis M

a

FIG. 34.—Drapery in the Style of the Archaic
Statues in the Acropolis Museum, Athens.

b

FIG. 35.—Vase-painting—British Museum.

FIG. 39.—Fragments of a Sarcophagus Cover from Kertch

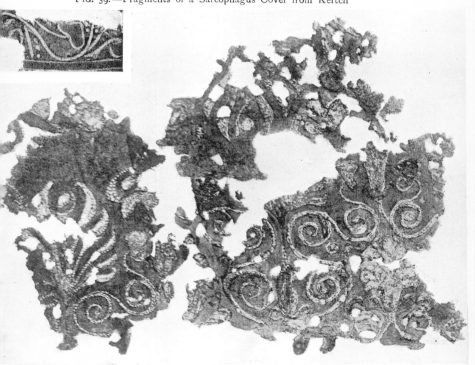

FIG. 40.—Embroidered Fragment from Kertch.

PLATE V

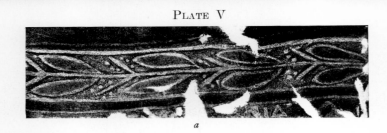

a

b

c

FIG. 41.—(*a* and *b*) Fragments of a Sarcophagus Cover from Kertch.
(*c*) Embroidered Fragment from Kertch.

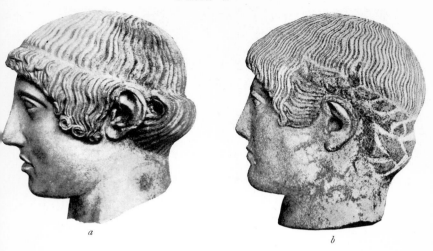

FIG. 43.—(a) Head of Apollo from the Temple of Zeus, at Olympia.
(b) Head of an Athlete—Athens Acropolis Museum.

FIG. 48.—(a) A Bronze in the British Museum. (b) Foot of the Hermes
of Praxiteles (from a cast in the British Museum). (c) A Terra-cotta
Flask in the British Museum.

PLATE X

FIG. 52.—(a) A Pyxis in the British Museum. (b) A Toilet-box in the British Museum.

FIG. 53.—(a) Bronze Box Mirror—British Museum. (b) Bronze Stand Mirror—British Museu

V

THE MAIDENS OF THE ACROPOLIS

THE DEVELOPMENT OF THE IONIC HIMATION

THE problem of the drapery of the archaic female figures in the Acropolis Museum has been considered by various archæologists, but has not yet been satisfactorily solved in all its details by any of them. The questions to be decided are : Firstly, are we to suppose that the draperies of the statues give us a faithful and realistic reproduction of a costume actually in fashion among the Athenian ladies at the close of the sixth century, or must we take into account the fact that the work is still archaic and the artists have not yet sufficiently mastered their material to be able to reproduce exactly what they saw before them ? Secondly, what are the separate garments which constitute the elaborately complicated whole ? And thirdly, how are these garments arranged so as to produce the effect seen in the statues ?

The answer to our first question is to be found in a compromise lying somewhere between the two hypotheses suggested. The early artist, struggling

K

with the technical difficulties of his art, is always
ready, as soon as he has solved one problem to his
satisfaction, to pass on to something which presents
still greater difficulties and demands the exercise of
still greater skill.   The makers of the Acropolis
maidens have advanced so far as to be able to
infuse some sort of life into their work ;—witness the
lively expression on some of the faces.   Moreover,
in the modelling of some parts of the human figure
they have reached a high degree of excellence.   In
the few cases in which the feet of the statues are
preserved, a great degree of delicacy and refinement is displayed, which shows that the artists
had attained some considerable power over their
material.   Having advanced so far, they feel themselves equal to facing the problem of representing
drapery in sculpture.   It is not to be supposed that
at this stage of artistic development they would
invent difficulties which did not naturally present
themselves, nor would they attempt to represent
anything that they had not actually seen ; therefore,
we must conclude that the Athenian ladies of the
period actually wore a dress corresponding closely
to that reproduced in art.   At the same time, it
must be remembered that the Greek artist in all
probability did not work with a model constantly
before him, so that we must expect some slight
differences in detail on that account ; furthermore,
we must make some allowance for archaism ; for
example, in all the statues under discussion, the
drapery does not fall freely away from the figure,

but follows the lines of the form beneath in a manner impossible in real life.

Having determined that the artists have represented a dress which was actually worn, we must proceed to consider the character of the dress as a whole, and of the parts of which it consisted. In giving a general description it will be best to take an example which exhibits all, or nearly all, the characteristics that can be collected from the various statues. No. 594 will serve our purpose. (Perrot and Chipiez, pl. xii. ; Lechat, *Au Musée de l'Acropole*, fig. 16.)[1] The under-garment which appears on the neck and left arm is represented by a series of fine wavy lines, running parallel to one another, which give a crinkled appearance, and may possibly be meant to indicate a material which has undergone some special treatment in the making. This garment is finished at the neck and down the upper part of the arm by an ornamental border, originally painted, but from which the colour has now almost entirely disappeared. The lower part of the figure is covered by a very long and ample garment, which I shall hope to prove to be the same as that which covers the left shoulder and upper arm. This garment is ornamented with a broad and elaborate meander pattern down the middle of the front ; and if the statue were not broken, we should probably see another border round the bottom. So far, the costume is comparatively simple ; but above this

[1] Fig. 31.

under-garment is worn a cloak which passes under the left arm and is drawn up to the right shoulder, where it is fastened so as to hang in heavy vertical folds down the right-hand side of the figure, back and front; in most cases we shall find that the cloak is fastened by a series of buttons along the upper part of the arm, as far as the curve of the elbow. The example before us now has an additional wrap, which conceals the fastening down the right arm. The rest of the cloak, passing under the left arm, hangs in a series of oblique but almost vertical folds, running parallel to a box-pleat which starts from the shoulder. These folds are apparently held in place by a band passing under the left arm and fixed on the other shoulder. The upper edge of the cloak hangs over this band in a sort of little frill with a zigzag edge. The mass of folds lying close to the figure under the left arm represents the material which forms the sleeve of the chiton. The additional wrap seen in one or two of the statues is a very simple matter; it consists of a large scarf worn over the shoulders, hanging down to a point on the left-hand side; it leaves the left arm uncovered, passes round the back, and over the right shoulder. Instead of hanging straight down to a point in the right-hand side, the end of the scarf is turned up and thrown over the arm. The end is broken away in No. 594, but appears in another instance (No. 684, Acropolis Museum; Perrot and Chipiez, fig. 297, p. 592). Both cloak and scarf are bordered with patterns, of which the colour still remains to some extent.

Many theories have been advanced as to the various garments which compose the costume. It will be well to give a brief summary of them, and to point out wherein they fall short, and, if possible, to substitute one that is more satisfactory.

The chief point at issue is whether the skirt part of the drapery belongs to the chiton—that is to say, to the garment which appears on the neck and left arm—or whether it is part of the cloak which passes under the left arm and is fastened on the right shoulder. Collignon even distinguishes three garments; he believes that the skirt is the chiton proper, and that the crinkled texture of the piece which appears above the himation is meant to represent some sort of woollen jersey worn over the chiton, which he calls the "chitoniscus."

The difference in texture comes out very plainly in those cases where the himation is worn over the shoulders like a shawl, or where it is omitted altogether; for example, in Nos. 670 and 671.[1]

At first sight it appears as though two separate garments were intended, but on close examination it will be found that the curved line which terminates the wavy lines of the upper section has not the appearance of an edge, but appears rather to turn under and to represent a pouch, formed by pulling the garment up through the girdle. Moreover, in

[1] Lechat, figs. 8 and 9 ; Perrot and Chipiez, 290 and 292.

some cases these parallel wavy lines appear on the skirt as well, and cover the whole surface with the exception of the mass of folds hanging down the middle of the front.   This can clearly be seen in No. 687 (Lechat, p. 161), in a small statue of the same type from Eleusis, now in the National Museum, Athens, and in the relief of the Charites in the Acropolis Museum (Lechat, pl. 3).   Again, the same technique is found sometimes introduced into the rendering of the himation.   Frequently on the shoulder, when the cloak is fastened, a succession of these wavy parallel lines begins to appear, then stops suddenly, and the rest of the garment presents a smooth surface.[1]   There can be no question here of a difference of material, nor of a separate piece of drapery, so that we must look for some other explanation of the different treatment.   Lechat has offered one which is satisfactory and which finds confirmation in other monuments.   He says "the difference in the appearance of the upper and lower part of the same garment is due to this : that in the lower part, all the superfluous material is gathered together in a single mass, and the rest is drawn tightly across the legs ; while in the upper part, the material, being left free, falls in regular folds all round the body."   He further suggests that the regularity of the folds may be meant to represent some artificial treatment of the dress, such as is applied to the modern *fustanella*.   The archaism of the work, however, is sufficient to account for this

[1] See Fig. 32.

regularity in representing a series of very full folds
in a fine material held in rather closely to the figure.
The same kind of treatment appears on many of
the red-figured vases of the best period.   One from
a vase by Euphronios is reproduced by Kalkmann
(*Jahrbuch*, vol. ix.) ; it occurs also on the well-known
Troilus vase by the same artist, and in numerous
other instances (Klein, *Euphronios*, p.   215).
Above the girdle the folds are represented by fine
parallel wavy lines drawn very close together
below by straight lines.   In these cases there is no
questioning the fact that only one garment is
intended, so that we may conclude that in the case
of the Acropolis statues too, there is no need to
suppose that the difference in texture represents
two separate garments of different materials.

It has been suggested that there may be an
intention on the part of the artist to indicate some
kind of material that had a crinkled texture, such as
that of some of the modern Greek stuffs ; but if
this were so, we might reasonably expect to find the
same technique all over the garment, and the
comparison with the vases shows that the supposi-
tion is not necessary.

We may conclude, then, that in those cases
where the himation is omitted altogether, the
figure is draped in a single garment, namely, the
long Ionic chiton described above.

In the case of these statues, the chiton is
exceptionally long ; there is still some material left
trailing on the ground after the formation of the

deep "kolpos," which necessitates the skirt being held up in one hand, so as not to impede walking. We are at once reminded of the Ἰάονες Ἑλκεχιτῶνες of the Homeric Hymn to Apollo.

We have next to consider those cases—and they are in the majority—where another garment is worn over the chiton; and it is on this point that archæologists are at variance. Many maintain that the chiton only appears on the upper left-hand side of the figure, and that a very large cloak is worn over it, which covers the whole of the rest of the chiton, and has a deep overfold at the top and trails on the ground behind, being held up in front and drawn aside in the left hand. Studniczka supports this view, and calls the garment an "ionisirende Peplos." Holwerda, in an article in the *Jahrbuch* for 1904, gives some drawings of some practical experiments he has made in draping a model in a garment of this kind. He supposes that it is cylindrical in shape, with a deep overfold, which is shorter on the shoulder than elsewhere, and so produces a zigzag line along its lower edge when draped; a girdle is worn underneath the overfold, through which the superfluous length left by shortening the overfold on the shoulder can be drawn. He supposes that the garment was drawn tightly round under the left arm, and that its upper edge formed the frill which we see in many of the Acropolis statues. A comparison between his finished model and the statue which he reproduces beside it serves to show the points wherein his theory falls short; it in

no way accounts for the vertical folds of the cloak,
nor for the tight band which appears passing
under the left arm and fastened on the right
shoulder. Amelung, writing in Pauly-Wissowa's
Real Encyclopädie, and Professor E. A. Gardner, in
his *Handbook of Greek Sculpture*, maintain that the
garment is simply a Doric peplos fastened on one
shoulder instead of both, and held in place by a
tight band, under which the width of the peplos is
arranged in vertical folds. The main objections to
to this theory are that the Doric peplos is invariably fastened in one place only on the shoulder,
whereas the fastening of the garment in question is
continued by a series of brooches down as far as
the elbow; the result would be to leave a very
heavy and cumbersome mass of material hanging
from the right arm, which would seriously impede
any active motion. Moreover, it leaves out of
account a piece of material which appears almost
invariably in front, below the zigzag edge, where it is
drawn up highest.[1] Holwerda takes it to be a
girdle, but it has not the appearance of a girdle;
it hangs over the material that falls from below it,
and does not cut into the soft stuff in the way in
which a girdle would. That the makers of these
statues knew how to represent a girdle is plain from
No. 679,[2] where the Doric peplos is worn over the
Ionic chiton. In this case the peplos is consider-

---

[1] Perrot and Chipiez, VIII., pls. 5 and 12.; Lechat, 22, 29, 30, etc.
This feature comes out clearly in fig. 31.
[2] Perrot and Chipiez, VIII., fig. 303 ; Lechat, fig. 31.

ably shorter than the chiton, so that the latter garment is plainly seen below the peplos, which only hangs down to a distance somewhat above the ankles. The Caryatid of the Cnidian Treasury at Delphi has the girdle clearly represented below the box-pleat by two parallel, horizontal, incised lines. On the frieze of the same building some of the figures are represented wearing the Doric peplos as an over-garment ; in these cases also it is shorter than the chiton, which invariably appears below it at the feet. An archaic statue from Rhamnus, in Attica, now in the British Museum, has the crinkly chiton showing at the feet, and over it a himation with a deep overfold reaching considerably below the waist ; in addition to this overfold a pleated frill appears over the breast, but no band is visible ; the frill, however, is deeper than is usually the case in the Acropolis statues, and might be intended to conceal a band. This over-dress is sewn up at the side, and in that respect resembles the Doric peplos. It is significant that in this case, where the garment might with more reason be regarded as a Doric peplos let down from one shoulder, the chiton is seen appearing below it at the feet, and the over-dress does not reach to the ankles. In the few cases where the feet of the Acropolis statues are preserved, it will be noticed that the skirt is held up fairly high towards one side, so as to display the ankle. If a long under-garment were worn, we should expect its lower edge to be seen here ; but in no instance is that the case, so that we may conclude that the skirt itself is the under-garment. Those who maintain that the skirt belongs to the upper garment support their opinion by the fact that very frequently the ornamentation on the two different parts is the same; the natural colour of the marble is left as a ground, and the decoration consists of coloured borders and patterns dotted somewhat sparsely over the surface. The part of the dress which appears on the left shoulder is frequently painted all over, and we might have expected that if the skirt belonged to the same garment it would also be painted all over. But before accepting this argument as conclusive, it will be well to consider the nature and purpose of polychromy as applied to Greek sculpture.

In the early days when inferior materials were used for sculpture, colour was applied to them to conceal the poverty of the stone and to produce a more pleasing surface than that offered by the rough material at the artist's disposal. These coarser materials were not capable of such careful finish, or of producing such a lively play of light and shade, as the marbles later used, and the only way to give them animation was by the application of colour all over the surface. It became, therefore, a regular practice for early Greek sculptors to paint their statues. When, however, they began to use more beautiful materials, such as marble, they recognised that it was a pity to conceal its texture by the extensive application of colour. They therefore adopted the practice of submitting the surface of the marble to a process of polishing, and adding colour only in parts, the effect being that the beauty of the marble is enhanced by the contrast between its polished surface and the coloured parts of the statue. The range of colours used is somewhat limited and conventional. For example, in the early pediment groups from the Acropolis, we find red used for human flesh; and the colours used in the draperies of the Acropolis female statues are limited to red and blue. Both eyes and hair are invariably red. We may infer, therefore, that colour was not added with a view to reproducing nature faithfully, but simply to decorate the statues. If, therefore, the artist felt that a white surface of marble with a few patterns sprinkled over it produced a more pleasing effect than a surface coloured all over, he would use this method of decorating his work, even if it were not realistic; and he would prefer to treat large surfaces of drapery in this way, rather than colour them all over. When, therefore, in these statues, we find that the small surface of the chiton which appears on the upper part of the figure is coloured all over, we need not conclude that the skirt belongs to another garment because it is differently ornamented; had so large a surface been painted all over, the effect would have been far less pleasing. The difference in the decoration of different parts of the same garment need in no way surprise us; it occurs very frequently in the black-figured vases, where we get purple used for the upper part of a garment and black for the lower, simply with the object of producing variety. The argument from the application of coloured ornament will not help us, then, in this case, especially when we find that it can be used to support either view. Professor Baldwin Brown has pointed out that some terra-cotta figures [1] in the Acropolis Museum, which are draped in the same style as the archaic statues, have the under-garment covering the shoulder and the skirt painted in one colour, and the part which passes round the figure under the left arm in another, and he uses this fact as a piece of evidence to show that the skirt is part of the chiton and the rest a separate garment.[2] It will be safer, therefore, in considering the different garments which constitute the dress, to leave the question of colour out of account altogether, and to base our arguments only on their form. Many who maintain that the skirt is part of the chiton, are of the opinion that the upper garment is the ordinary himation with a small over-fold, fastened on the shoulder and down the arm. Lechat supposes that the upper edge is taken up and drawn from beneath and folded over on itself, so as to form a sort of thick pad at the top, and he suggests that the pleats were folded before the cloak was put on, and perhaps even ironed; but this arrangement would not produce the vertical folds which we find in almost all the statues.

[1] Cp. *Jahrbuch*, 1893 ; Arch. Anz., H. 519 ; Winter.
[2] Another possibility which suggests itself is that the sculptor may not have painted the statue himself, but may have handed it over to a painter who did not understand how the drapery was constituted.

Kalkmann[1] calls the garment a "stilisirte himation," and suggests that the vertical lines are continued round the figure because the artist had great difficulty in representing the transition between the vertical folds which hang down from the arm and the horizontal ones of the overfold. This explanation, however, does not account for the frill-like edge which appears at the top of the himation. Professor Baldwin Brown[2] has published some good photographs of a model draped in this Ionian himation, but has not given a very full or satisfactory explanation of how the effect was produced. He says that the secret of the dress is that "the upper edge of it, with all the folds, is tightly rolled over so that it is shortened in the front, while at the same time the folds are kept in their places." He admits that the folds will only keep in place on a "motionless wearer of imperturbable patience," and therefore supposes that the dress was evolved for use on the wooden xoana. It seems unlikely that a special dress of such an elaborate nature should have been evolved to drape these early wooden images, and there is no reason to suppose that the series of Acropolis statues are merely reproductions of such images. They appear much rather to represent the grand Athenian ladies who dedicated themselves symbolically to their patron goddess by setting up statues of themselves in her honour. Since the statues were probably intended to be set up permanently in a conspicuous

[1] *Jahrbuch*, xi.   [2] *How Greek Women Dressed.*

place, it is natural that the votaries would like to
see themselves appearing in their best clothes.

A careful study of the statues themselves and a
consideration of all the evidence bearing on the
question leads to the conclusion that the complete
costume consists of two garments, a long under-
dress, which may be regarded as the usual indoor
costume of the Athenian ladies of the sixth century,
and a mantle worn over it for out of doors ; occasionally a scarf or shawl is worn as well over the
mantle, perhaps for additional warmth, perhaps only
for ornament.   The under-dress consists of the
long linen Ionic chiton, a wide cylindrical garment
fastened by brooches or sewn down both arms so
as to form sleeves ; a girdle is worn round the waist,
and the superfluous length of the material is drawn
up over this girdle so as to form a deep pouch ;
sometimes this pouch is worn all round the figure,
sometimes, as is apparently the case in a large
seated figure of Athena, the pouch is formed only
in front.   On some occasions[1] we find that the
chiton, in addition to the pouch, has an overfold
from the neck resembling the ἀπόπτυγμα of the
Doric peplos. This overfold sometimes only covers
the chest and sometimes hangs down considerably
lower. Such an overfold is very frequently found on
vases ; in some cases its material may be of one piece
with that of the rest of the chiton, as it appears on
one of the Nereids from the so-called Nereid monument ; but in those many cases where it only appears

[1] *E.g.*, Lechat, fig. 12.

between the shoulders and does not extend also along the arms, it is quite possible that it may be a separate piece of stuff sewn on to the chiton at the neck. It is probably the edge of such an overfold that appears at the waist below the himation on the Acropolis statues ; no other satisfactory explanation of this detail of the costume has at present been suggested. It is unlikely that it represents the "kolpos," because in all cases, with one possible exception (No. 676 ; Lechat, fig. 29), a border is painted on it, indicating that it is an edge and not a pouch. It has been suggested that this overfold was sometimes made of a different kind of material from the chiton on to which it was sewn, and that this material was a silk or linen of a crinkled texture, indicated by the wavy parallel lines which appear on the statues. The fact that this treatment appears sometimes also on the skirt and on the upper part of the mantle, diminishes the probability of this hypothesis, and makes it appear more likely that this kind of technique was simply used to represent very full folds in a fine material. Such a treatment may have been suggested to the artist by familiarity with some material of a crinkled texture, such as that used for sheets and table-cloths in some Greek villages to-day.

With regard to the ornamental patterns which adorn the chiton, we find borders at the feet and at the edge of the overfold, also strips of ornamentation running round the neck and along the arms and round the arm-holes, and almost invariably a broad band running vertically down the front of the lower part of the chiton.   In addition to these strips and borders we also get stars or small floral designs scattered over the whole garment.   The bands which appear at the edges are easy to understand ; they were either woven in the material of which they were made, or, more probably, embroidered on to it afterwards ; but in those cases where the over-fold is worn and a pattern appears at its edge and also along the neck and arms, we must suppose that this latter was applied after the sleeves were formed and the overfold attached.   Possibly, also, the vertical band on the lower part of the chiton represents a separate strip of embroidery sewn on to the garment.   The Greek women probably occupied a large proportion of their time in embroidery ; and since a good piece of embroidery lasts for very many years, it is quite possible that when the original garment was worn out, they may have cut off the strip of still good work, and sewn it on to a new dress.   The only other explanation of the numerous patterns which appear on the statues, is that the artist simply applied ornamentation wherever it pleased his fancy to do so ; this is less satisfactory than to suppose that he was representing something which he actually saw.

Turning to the himation or mantle worn over the chiton, the simplest method of producing the effect seen in the Acropolis statues was found by experiment to be by taking a piece of material between 5 and 6 yards long and about 18 or 20

M

inches wide. This was folded double, as in the diagram at the point *a*, so that the points *b* and *b'* met. Then at the points *c* and *c'*, at equal distances from the corners, and cutting off at little less than one-third of the wide length of the stuff, the two upper edges were fastened together on the model's right shoulder, a few pleats or gathers being taken in the material on each side. A series of such fastenings was made along the upper arm, as far as the points *d* and *d'*, which reached to the model's elbow ; the rest of the stuff, as far as the points *b* and *b'*, was allowed to hang down from the elbow. The

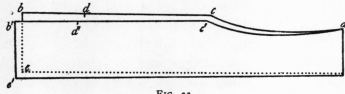

FIG. 33.

part of the material *c* to *c'* passed under the left arm and was arranged in a series of regular oblique folds running parallel to the box-pleat, which formed itself naturally at the first fastening on the shoulder—that is to say, at the points *c* and *c'* ; these folds were held in place by a band passing under the left breast, drawn rather tightly round the figure and secured firmly on the right shoulder. In order to make the lower edge of the cloak rise in the middle, as it does invariably in the statues, it was found necessary to draw the folds up over the band and let the upper edge fall over, forming a kind of frill. The frill, however, hung down too low, and it was this fact that suggested cutting the upper edge of the cloak out in a curve, or rather in two curves, one at the back and one at the front, leaving the part under the left arm longer than that in front and behind. When these curves were cut out and the garment once more arranged in its pleats, the little frill-like edge hung of itself over the band, just in the way in which it appears in some of the statues. The band alone held the folds fairly well in place ; but in order to prevent the possibility of their slipping, the Athenian ladies probably had them stitched on to the band. It would be quite easy to slip the garment on and off over the head without even unfastening it on the shoulder.[1]

The variations in detail which appear in the different statues can easily be produced by arranging the folds in a slightly different fashion. In some cases, as for example in No. 674 (Lechat, pl. 1), the folds hang quite upright instead of obliquely, and the box-pleat appears in the middle instead of hanging from the shoulder ; this can easily be produced by turning the folds first in one direction and then in the opposite. The folds of the frill sometimes hang in the opposite direction to those of the main part of the mantle ; this is simply a mistake on the part of the artist. Occasionally the frill does not appear at all, for example in No. 686 (Lechat, fig. 37), but the cloak hangs straight down from the broad band. In this instance we must

[1] Figs. 34, *a* and *b*, are photographs of a model draped in this manner.

suppose that the overhanging mass of material has been cut away entirely before the folds were attached to the band.

Sometimes the two ends were sewn together along the lines be and $b'e'$, and in this case the last fastening, indicated by the letters d and d', approached nearer to the points b and b', so as to leave an opening only sufficient for the arm to pass through.

The detail of the cloak which presents most variety is the little frill-like edge which falls over the band. Sometimes it appears to be a natural continuation of the vertical folds which hang down below it, and it falls over the band so as almost to hide it; sometimes it is shorter, and reveals the band and forms a sort of leaf-like pattern above it; in other cases it disappears entirely. Its most realistic representation is in one of the Victories in the Acropolis Museum, where the corners c and c', formed by cutting the curves, are actually indicated on the shoulder, and the frill lies in an irregular zigzag, almost exactly as it was found to fall in practice.

In two cases in the Acropolis Museum at Athens, and in a statue at Delphi, the band does not pass under the arm, but from shoulder to shoulder, and the cloak covers both arms symmetrically, being fastened down both alike with a series of brooches. In these cases the box-pleat falls in the middle, and the curve must necessarily have been considerably smaller, since the upper edge lies much higher up towards the neck. When the cloak was worn in this way, it was probably sewn up down both sides, and the curves for the neck, back and front, were naturally equidistant from the two side-seams. The openings for the arms would come at the ends of the top edge, as in the case of the Ionic chiton.

The style of dress represented by this set of monuments is certainly the most luxurious which we find in Greek art at any period. Now the date of the Acropolis maidens can be fixed at some period certainly not later than the last quarter of the sixth century. Solon's sumptuary law regulating women's dress must have been enacted during the first years of the sixth century, so that we may conclude that these dainty ladies with their chitons, cloaks, and scarfs represent the height of luxury in dress which was possible after the passing of that law : their self-satisfied smile seems to be inviting approval of the degree of elegance to which their ingenuity could attain, even though a stern law-giver had limited the number of their garments to three.

This style of dress seems to have passed out of fashion at the end of the sixth century, or in the early years of the fifth, for we find it only in the early works of sculpture already mentioned. An attempt to render it is frequently made by the artists of the early red-figured vases—sometimes with some success ; but more often the attempt results in a confusion between this somewhat elaborate style of cloak and the simpler development which it took later. Fig. 35 shows a fairly successful attempt to represent the dress. Here we have the band passing round the right shoulder and the vertical folds falling from it, but the frill and the fastening down the right arm are omitted. Possibly they taxed the artist's skill too greatly; possibly the style had already passed out of fashion in real life. But he would be moderately familiar with the maidens on the Acropolis, although perhaps not sufficiently so to be able to reproduce their costume in detail. Working daily in his little shop down below in the Cerameicus, perhaps he did not very frequently mount the citadel, where he might study the art treasures that adorned it. Possibly even the vase is not earlier than 480 B.C., and the picture is but a reminiscence of the statues that the artist had seen on the Acropolis previous to their burial at the coming of the Persians. Very often on the vases we find the vertical folds represented falling from beneath a series of horizontal folds obviously formed by turning over the top of the cloak before fastening it on the shoulder. Here the band and fastening down the arm are omitted.[1] The place of the frill is taken by an overfold of the cloak before it is put on, and it is fastened by a single brooch on the shoulder; the material is allowed to hang in natural folds, and the necessity of cutting a curve in the upper edge is obviated by the fact that no band is worn, and the stuff is not arranged in artificial vertical folds. This style of cloak appears already on the figure of Apollo, on the relief from Thasos in the Louvre; it is seen most clearly in

[1] Fig. 36.

the Artemis of Gabii.[1] It was probably developed from the earlier and more elaborate form of cloak by gradual stages, first by omitting the artificial folds and the band which held them in place, and then by omitting the numerous fastenings on the arm. This would necessitate an alteration in the shape of the cloak; it would naturally become more square. Kalkmann, in the article already referred to, fig. 17, represents an intermediate stage in this development, where a large cloak is worn without band or frill, and is fastened by a series of several brooches down one arm.   Were it not for this representation of the transition stage, we might be inclined to class the cloak of the Artemis of Gabii as a development of the Doric peplos, which it resembles in having an overfold and being fastened by a single large brooch on the shoulder ; and indeed these two elements are probably due to the influence of the Doric dress, and we should therefore, perhaps, more rightly call the final form of the cloak a blending of the two styles rather than a development of either the one or the other.

As early as the beginning of the fifth century we find the two styles becoming confused and mingled together.   The Doric peplos is worn as an over-dress over the Ionic chiton, even by one of the " Maidens " of the Acropolis, and later on the commonest form of outdoor dress for women was the Ionic chiton with the Doric himation over it. This combination appears in the so-called Fates of the Parthenon pediment.   Frequently we find this

[1] Fig. 37.

blending of the two styles in a single garment; we find also on vases the overgirt Doric peplos with sleeves formed by a number of brooches;[1] and again, with cross-bands, which belong properly to the Ionic chiton.[2]   Some authorities, pinning their faith entirely to Herodotus, consider that the the brooch is an element which belongs strictly only to the Doric dress; they therefore regard the chiton with pinned sleeves as a mixture of the two. An over-garment not very simple in form, which can be regarded as neither Doric nor Ionic, but a mixture of both, is illustrated by Fig. 38.   Kalkmann regards it as a number of overfolds or flounces sewn separately on to the chiton.   It seems more reasonable, however, to regard the part of the dress which appears on the arms and at the feet, and which is made of a plain material, as the chiton, and the rest which is ornamented with a pattern, as a separate over-garment.   This garment has three edges, at the waist, hips, and ankles, so that it is obviously not merely an ordinary rectangular himation, nor a simple Doric peplos with overfold. It seems simplest to explain it as a Doric peplos with deep overfold, ungirt, having a short false overfold to the waist sewn on over the real one at the neck.   Such over-garments never occur in sculpture and only rarely on the vases, and may possibly be an error or invention on the part of the vase-painter; if commonly worn, they would probably be more frequently represented in art.

[1] B.M., E. 336.   [2] Athens Central Museum, 1285.

VI

MATERIALS AND ORNAMENTATION

The fabrics in use for Greek dresses presented considerable variety. The commonest materials were naturally woollen, but linen and silk were used for more luxurious garments, and a kind of leather jerkin known as διφθέρα[1] was sometimes worn by peasants.

That the woollen materials used themselves varied considerably in texture, is proved by some fragments actually found in a tomb at Kertch in the Crimea, and published in the *Comptes rendus* in 1878. These date for the most part from the fourth century B.C., but one at least probably goes back to the fifth century. They are in most cases rather loosely woven, so that the separate threads are clearly visible, and a bright object could be seen through the material. The oldest piece is composed of such fine threads that it is almost transparent; other pieces have a texture not unlike that of woollen crêpe. A somewhat coarser piece, the threads of which are very strong, has a portion of a seam remaining, which is oversewn with strong

[1] Aristophanes, *The Clouds*, 72 ; Plato, *Crito*, 53 D.

woollen thread. In addition to very finely woven woollen materials, the more luxurious of the Greeks wore also many varieties of linen, and in some cases even silk. Pollux tells us that the long linen chiton was worn by the Athenians and Ionians, and many references are to be found in ancient literature to different kinds of linen, coming from places usually in Asia or the more easterly of the Ægean islands. Of these the most commonly mentioned are ἀμόργινα, garments made of linen from the flax of Amorgos, and βύσσινα, made of βύσσος, a yellowish kind of flax, coming especially from India and Egypt. We learn from Aristophanes [1] that the χιτώνιον ἀμόργινον was transparent, so that we may conclude that the linen from which it was made was very fine indeed; perhaps it resembled a very fine cambric. That βύσσος was a linen of some kind, we are told by Pausanias,[2] and Pollux gives us the information that it came from India. That it was known in Egypt also, is testified by Herodotus,[3] who tells us of its use for mummy-cloths. It was probably rather a mark of luxury when worn by the Greeks, for Simætha [4] tells us that she wore a χιτών of it when going out on a festive occasion.

Of materials which come under the heading of silk, three kinds were known to the ancients. We read in Latin authors of *vestes coæ, bombycinæ,* and *sericæ,* and these were also known to the Greeks. Aristotle [5] is the first of the ancient writers who

---

[1] *Lys.,* 150.   [2] VI., 21.   [3] II., 86.
[4] Theocritus, II., 73.   [5] *Hist. Anim.,* v., 19.

tells us anything of the production of silk. After
describing the various changes undergone by the
worm before becoming a moth, he gives us the
following information :—

Ἐκ δὲ τούτου τοῦ ζῴου καὶ τὰ βομβύκια ἀναλύουσι τῶν
γυναικῶν τινές ἀναπηνιζόμεναι, κἄπειτα ὑφαίνουσιν · πρώτη δὲ
λέγεται ὑφῆναι ἐν Κῷ Παμφίλη Πλάτεω θυγάτηρ.

"Some women undo the cocoons of this creature,
winding off the silk, and then weave it; and
Pamphile, daughter of Plateus, is said to have been
the first to weave it in Cos." This implies that the
manufacture of silk was carried on in Cos, but no
information is given as to whether the worm was
reared in that island or whether the raw silk was
imported. Pliny[1] tells us more on the subject; he
seems to distinguish the three kinds of silk
mentioned above. Of these three, only "sericum"
is, strictly speaking, silk—that is to say, a material
made by unwinding the cocoon of the silkworm
reared on the mulberry tree. This worm is first
mentioned by Pausanias.[2] It was the Chinese who
discovered this method of procuring the silk, and it
was apparently unknown to the Greeks and Romans.
The "coa" and "bombycina" were procured
by piercing and carding the cocoon instead of
unwinding them entire; the result was a substance
coarser and less brilliant than silk. Pliny draws a
distinction between "coa" and "bombycina," telling
us that the latter was a product of Assyria and
came from the ordinary mulberry worm, whereas the

[1] *Hist. Nat.*, xi.   [2] VI., xxvi., 6.

worm from which coan silk was procured was reared on other trees, notably the oak, ash, and cypress.[1]

Coæ vestes are frequently mentioned by the Latin poets, chiefly Horace, Tibullus, and Propertius, and from them we learn that they were chiefly worn by *Hetairæ* and were of a transparent texture ;[2] sometimes they were purple and had gold threads interwoven or embroidered.[3] One piece of silk was found amongst other materials at Kertch. In colour it is a bronze-gold, and is woven in a lozenge pattern.

If Greek dress lacked variety of cut and material, the deficiency was to some extent made up by considerable gaiety of colour and ornamentation. Probably none but slaves and artisans would wear garments of one colour without pattern or ornamentation of any kind, and even they would sometimes have their dresses adorned with a simple border, such as a broad stripe. From the numerous references scattered up and down through extant literature, it appears that the favourite colours were purple, red, and yellow. Pollux[4] gives us a list of the colours most commonly used. This list includes green (βατραχίς) and gray (κίλλιον, ὀνάγρινον), in addition to those mentioned above, but strangely enough no mention is made of blue. The word

---

[1] For silk generally, see Daremberg and Saglio, *s.v.* "coa"; Smith, *Dictionary of Antiquities, s.v.* "sericum"; Yates, *Textrinum Antiquorum*, pp. 160 f. ; Pariset, *Histoire de la Soie*, Part I., chap. i.

[2] Propertius, I., 2 ; Horace, *Satires*, I., ii., 101.

[3] Horace, *Odes*, IV., xiii. ; Tibullus, II., 6.   [4] Chap. lviii.

κυάνεος, "dark blue," is seldom if ever applied to
garments, yet it is scarcely likely that the colour
was unknown to the Greeks. Possibly some shades
described as πορφύρεος approached a violet, or blue,
as distinguished from ἀλούργος, "true purple." For
red we find the word φοινίκεος, "dark red," used
especially of the military cloak of the Lacedæmonians,[1] and κοκκοβαφής, "scarlet"; for yellow
κροκωτός and θάψινος. Βατραχίς, "frog-coloured," is
the word applied to a green garment, and this
is probably the colour described as ὀμφάκινος, "like
unripe grapes." Pollux[2] tells us that for mourning
the Greeks wore φαιὸν καὶ μέλαν ἀλλήλοις ἔγγυς, "gray
and black, very like each other." From this we
learn that φαιός was a very dark colour, probably
gray or dun.

The ornamentation applied to dress by the
Greeks was very varied in character; it is comparatively rare to find on Greek vases a dress that
is entirely free from decorations, and the patterns
represented are very numerous. Sometimes the
ornament consists of a simple border, often of a
pattern distributed all over the dress, and these
designs are frequently of a very elaborate character,
including animal and even human forms. In
sculpture, too, this feature was not neglected; the
maidens of the Acropolis at Athens all have some
pattern on their draperies added in colour, and one
of them has no less than seven different designs
distributed over her costume. We know that the

[1] Aristophanes, *Pax*, 1173; *Lys.*, 1140.   [2] 58.

himation of the Olympian Zeus by Pheidias was richly decorated, and the fragment from Damophon's great group at Lycosura will serve as a later example of sculptured drapery highly ornamented with patterns in relief. This has not only geometric and floral designs as borders, but the whole surface is covered with fantastic dancing figures of human and hybrid forms.

References in literature are not very frequent; the most noteworthy occurs in the *Iliad*,[1] where Helen is described as working at a great loom :

> ἡ δὲ μέγαν ἱστὸν ὕφαινεν
> δίπλακα πορφυρέην, πολέας δ' ἐνέπασσεν ἀέθλους
> Τρώων θ' ἱπποδάμων καὶ 'Αχαιῶν χαλκοχιτώνων.

"She was weaving a great purple web of double fold, and over it she spread many battles of horse-taming Trojans and bronze-clad Achæans."

The epithet ποικίλος, applied to dress, undoubtedly means "richly decorated," and the ἀνθινά, "flowered garments," frequently mentioned in inscriptions, presumably refers to garments ornamented with floral designs. In connection with the passage in Homer, the question has been raised as to whether these complex designs were woven into the material or embroidered afterwards. It seems hardly likely that they were woven in, unless the work were a heavy tapestry, such as would hardly be suitable for a costume; moreover, the word ἐμπάσσω means "to sprinkle on," and is more easily applicable to the distribution of a design over a piece of material

[1] iii., 125.

already woven than to the formation of a pattern in the course of the weaving.   The words μέγαν, ἰστὸν, and ὕφαινεν would still be applicable, because when the garment was at this stage, it would still be regarded as incomplete, and the designs, however applied, would probably be at least sketched out while it was still on the loom.

Among the fragments of materials found at Kertch were some which were embroidered, others which had simple geometrical designs woven into the borders ; in addition to these there were some considerable fragments of a large sarcophagus cover, the ornamentation of which is strongly reminiscent of Greek vase-painting of the fourth century. The ground is black and is covered with designs in red and light terra-cotta ; the ornamentation is divided into bands, and consists of battle scenes with chariots, and birds and beasts scattered about the field of the design ; the bands are separated by different patterns, many of which are frequently met with on vases.   These include the egg and dart pattern, ivy and laurel wreaths, large palmettes, and many others.[1]   Names are inscribed against some of the figures, among others ΝΙΚΗ, ΑΘΗΝΑΙΗ ΙΟΚΑΣΤΗ, (Ι)ΠΠΟΜΕΔΩΝ, etc.

These designs are not embroidered, nor are they produced in the course of weaving the cloth ; they are apparently drawn out by means of some pigment applied after the material was woven. Herodotus tells us [2] that the people of the Caucasus

[1] Figs. 39 and 41 a and b.   [2] I., 203.

used to paint animals on their clothes with some
vegetable pigment which they mixed with water.
Some such procedure, then, must have been practised
by the Greeks of the fourth century, which is the
date assignable to the fragment in question, on the
evidence of the inscriptions.

The designs applied to Greek dresses presented
abundant variety, as is evidenced by extant monuments, especially by the vases ; they may be roughly
classed as geometric, floral, and those containing
animal and human forms.   Of the geometric designs
some are rectilinear, others curvilinear. The favourite
rectilinear borders are broad lines, parallel rows of
zigzag lines, the mæander or key pattern in very
many forms varying from the simple running
mæander to a complicated double fret, broken at
intervals by stars or chequers.   In addition to these
borders we frequently find a chequer pattern
covering the whole surface of a garment.   A kind
of net pattern, often seen on vases, was very probably
used in dresses also.   Of the curvilinear designs the
most common are the "guilloche" or plait-band,
the simple spiral, and the κυμάτιον or wave pattern.
On the black-figured vases a kind of scale pattern
frequently occurs covering a wide surface.

A very great variety of floral designs was used
by the Greeks for ornamentation of all kinds ; they
are very frequent as part of the scheme of decoration
of vases, especially of those of Ionic origin.   A
favourite pattern is a simple laurel wreath like that
depicted in Fig. 39 ; the ivy also forms the basis of

more than design. Sometimes it takes the form of a row of leaves on either side of a straight line; more often the leaves alternate with tendrils and berries. By far the commonest and the most beautiful of floral designs are those made up of lotus buds and flowers and palmettes. Sometimes we find the lotus alone forming the motive of the design, sometimes it alternates with palmettes. A very graceful pattern is composed of oblique palmettes turned in opposite directions and connected by spirals.[1] That these designs so commonly used for the decoration of pottery were employed also in the textile arts is proved by some of the fragments found at Kertch. Quite considerable remains were found of a piece of woollen material elaborately embroidered with a large floral design (Fig. 40), the main motive of which is a graceful palmette, from the base of which spring spirals terminating in heart-shaped leaves and flowers. The design is executed in gold and green on a violet ground.[2]

Animal and human forms are naturally less common than geometric and floral designs. Mention has already been made of the wonderful diplax woven by Helen, in which she represented scenes of battle between Trojans and Achæans. In art we find that goddesses are frequently depicted wearing garments covered with elaborate ornamentation of this kind. The François vase will afford several

[1] For patterns generally, see H. B. Walters, *History of Ancient Pottery*, ii., 209-235 ; Riegl, *Stilfragen*.
[2] For colouring, see *Comptes rendus*, 1878.

examples, and in later art the dress of Demeter on the Triptolemus vase by Hieron,[1] and the sculptured drapery from Damophon's group at Lycosura, may be quoted. That mortals also indulged in such luxurious ornamentation is proved again by the Kertch fragments. One of the most charming pieces found there had a very naturalistic design of ducks embroidered in gold and green on a dark-brown ground (Fig. 41 c); another piece had a figure of an Amazon riding on horseback; and mention has already been made of the sarcophagus cloth covered with battle scenes.

[1] British Museum, E. 140.   Fig. 14, above.

VII

HAIR AND HEAD-DRESS

THE manner of wearing the hair seems to have varied considerably at different periods, both for men and women. In pre-Hellenic times it was, for the most part, if not invariably, allowed to grow long. On the frescoes from Knossos we find the cupbearer and other male figures represented wearing their hair in long, wavy tresses reaching to the waist or thereabouts. On Mycenæan gems and rings, where warriors are represented wearing helmets, the hair is frequently concealed, so that it is impossible to determine whether it was worn short or bound up in some manner, so as to be out of the way. The ivory statuettes of athletes from Knossos have long hair,[1] so that in all probability that was the prevailing fashion among men in Crete. Among women in pre-Hellenic times, the fashion was to wear the hair long; the snake goddess and her votary have hair that reaches far past the waist, and in almost all extant art of the period the hair of the women is represented as being abundant. It is frequently worn in long tresses down the back

[1] See *British School Annual*, 1901-2, VIII., 72, fig. 37.

(compare the dancing girl, Fig. 4) and arranged
rather elaborately in front in curls, which sometimes
suggest artificial treatment ; sometimes the hair is
done up at the back or top of the head, in modern
fashion.

In'the Homeric poems we read of the "long-
haired Achæans,"[1] so that the sight of men with
long hair was obviously familiar to the poet.   From
the passage which describes Andromache's swoon,[2]
however, it is clear that the women of the poet's
day bound their hair up, using nets and kerchiefs
and other appurtenances both useful and ornamental.

Coming down to historic times, we find that
before the Persian wars both men and women wore
their hair long.   After the middle of the fifth century
a change took place, the men cutting their hair
short for the most part, the women binding it
up.   The story of the Lacedæmonians combing
their long hair when the Persians were close upon
them is familiar (Herodotus, VII., 208).   Extant
monuments show us that before the Persian wars the
men adopted various methods of disposing of their
long hair : sometimes we see it worn loose with a
simple fillet tied round the head ;[3] sometimes the
long ends are turned up and tucked in under the
fillet ;[4] sometimes they are turned up and held
together by an additional band.   This is the case
with a bronze head from Olympia,[5] where, however,
some locks seem to have been left free on the neck.

---

[1] *Iliad*, ii., 443, 472.   [2] *Ibid.*, xxii., 468 f.
[3] Fig. 42 (*a*).   [4] Fig. 42 (*b*).   [5] Fig. 42 (*c*).

A relief in Athens, representing a Discobolus holding the "discus" behind his head,[1] shows the hair probably divided and twisted together in two coils fastened tightly at a little distance from the end by a ribbon, or possibly by a metal spiral.[2] The golden τέττιξ mentioned by Thucydides (I., 6) was obviously some kind of ornament inserted in the hair to hold the "chignon" in place. It has been shown by Helbig[3] that this was probably a metal spiral or series of rings used to bind together the ends of the long hair; such a style is frequently represented in the art of the end of the sixth century and beginning of the fifth. The bands represented in Fig. 42 (c) are possibly intended for such metal rings. Helbig's view is supported and confirmed by Studniczka.[4]

Probably the knot of hair bound up on the nape of the neck, as in the above examples, represents the κρωβύλος or κόρυμβος mentioned in Thucydides and elsewhere in literature. In later times this name was applied to the knot of hair on the top of the head which occurs so frequently in statues of Apollo; but there is no evidence to show that it was worn in this position before the fourth century at the earliest.

A style very commonly exemplified by extant statues of Apollo, dating from the early part of the

[1] Fig. 42 (d).

[2] The hair of Euphorbus, described in *Iliad*, xvi., 52, was possibly dressed in this fashion.

[3] *Die Homerische Epos*, 166-170; cp. *Mittheilungen des Deutschen Instituts in Athen*, vi., pl. 7, p. 186.

[4] *Jahrbuch des kaiserlich Deutschen Instituts*, xi., 1896, pp. 284-291.

fifth century, is to tie a fillet round the head and roll the long hair tightly over it, tucking the ends in usually behind the ears.[1] These ends are, however, sometimes allowed to hang down on the neck. Athletes very frequently disposed of their long hair by braiding it into two plaits from behind; these they crossed or brought round the head, fastening the two ends together in front.[2] Sometimes the short hair in front was combed down over the plaits, so as to conceal their union.

The date of the change of fashion is impossible to fix. We find the athletes of Myron and Polycleitus represented with short hair, but long-haired Apollos are found considerably after their date. The change took place, in all probability, shortly after the Persian wars; it then became the fashion for Ephebi to cut off their long hair, which they consecrated to Apollo and Artemis or to a river god.[8] When once the change had come about, long hair was considered, in Athens at least, as a mark of affectation or effeminacy. In *The Wasps* of Aristophanes,[4] Amynias, the typical fop, is designated by the name of οὐκ τῶν Κρωβύλου, "he of the 'chignon,'" and in *The Clouds* the wearing of the τέττιξ is spoken of as a fashion quite out of date, or, as we might say, antediluvian. There is some uncertainty as to whether the Lacedæmonians wore their hair short or long; some authorities

[1] Fig. 43 (*a*).
[2] Fig. 43 (*b*). It is interesting to note that little Athenian schoolgirls of to-day wear their hair in this fashion.
[3] Pausanias, I., xxxvii., 2; Æsch. *Choeph.*, 6.   [4] 1267.

state that even in the fourth century they still wore it long as a mark of freedom, and since they were more conservative than the rest of the Greeks, it is quite possible that this was the case.   With this possible exception, the custom of wearing the hair short continued, though Alexander probably set the fashion of wearing rather long and mane-like hair.

A covering for the head was rarely worn by men, except when riding or travelling long distances ; in these cases the πέτασος was worn as a protection against sun and rain.   This consisted of a felt hat with broad brim, which could be turned up or down. Figs. 44, 22, and 23 represent its various shapes, Fig. 44 being the earliest form.   The πέτασος, like the χλάμυς, which it almost invariably accompanies, prob-

FIG. 44.

ably came originally from Northern Greece, Thrace, or Thessaly, where more protection was needed against cold and inclement weather.   Another head-covering, worn by sailors and by the god Hephaistos, is the πῖλος, a felt cap of conical shape resembling the modern fez.[1]

Extant monuments show that before the Persian wars women for the most part wore their hair down, although instances occur where it is fastened up with bands or fillets.   When worn down it was usually held in place by a fillet, and frequently a metal ornament, rather high in front and narrowing towards the back, was added.   This was known as

[1] Fig. 19.

the ἄμπυξ, or στεφάνη, and was probably made of gold; almost all the "Maidens" of the Acropolis wear it, and in several instances it is adorned with floral patterns.[1] The high πόλος or crown worn by Hera (Fig. 45 (a)) was probably also made of metal. Sometimes when the hair was worn down, the ends were prevented from flying in the wind by being tied together in a kind of little bag,[2] which reminds one of one of the many fashions adopted by men in the Georgian period in England. Sometimes, like the men, the women tucked the long ends up under the fillet, and let them hang out over it at the back. The fillet itself frequently assumed the dimensions of a scarf, the ends of which were tucked up at the sides and allowed to hang down behind the ears. When the hair was done up, the "chignon" was at first worn low on the nape of the neck and held in place by bands variously arranged.[3] Sometimes the στεφάνη alone was worn,[4] and very often the hair was held up by a kerchief or snood (μίτρα, σάκκος). The styles in which it was worn present abundant variety: sometimes it covered the hair completely,[5] except for a curl or two allowed to escape in front of the ears; sometimes it left the hair visible over the forehead only;[6] sometimes over the forehead and on the crown of the head, and the ends of the kerchief might be tucked through at the side and allowed to hang down in front of the ears.[7] Fig. 45 (f) gives an example of the στεφάνη worn in addition to

[1] Fig. 32.　　[2] Fig. 45 (b).　　[3] Fig. 45 (c and d).　　[4] Fig. 45 (e).
　　　[5] Fig. 45 (g).　　[6] Fig. 45 (h).　　[7] Fig. 45 (i and j).

FIG. 36.—Vase-painting—Ionic Dress.

FIG. 38.—Vase-painting—Dress with two Overfolds.

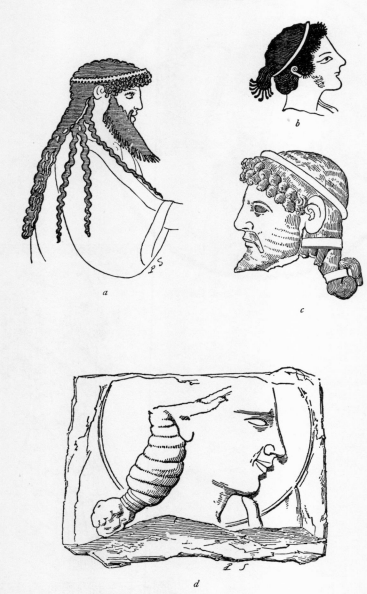

FIG. 42.—Men's Head-dress—Archaic.

FIG. 45.—Women's Head-dress.

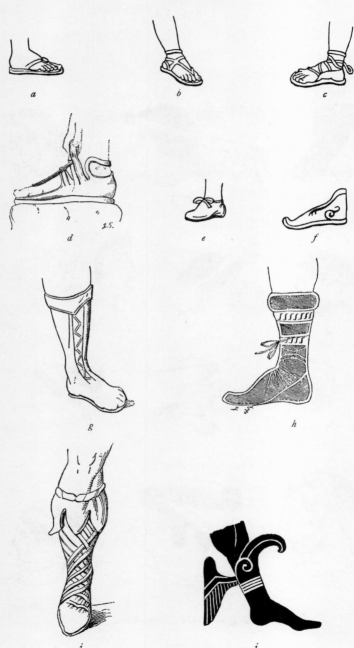

FIG. 46.—Sandals and Shoes.

the snood. In the fourth century fashion seems to
have dictated that the "chignon" should be worn
higher up at the back of the head, and a small
kerchief was used to hold it up, folded in such a
way that it narrowed almost to a point over the forehead.[1] Apparently a net was sometimes worn over
the back of the hair. Fig. 45 (*l*), from the Meidias
vase, furnishes an illustration of this. In Hellenistic
and Roman times the styles of dressing the hair
became very numerous. The snood seems to have
been discarded altogether, and adornment by means
of artificial waving and curling apparently took its
place. The modes of "coiffure" of the Alexandrian
Greeks are as varied as those of modern Europe.
Probably cosmetics were used for the hair and paint
and powder for the face ; for we learn from
Xenophon's *Œconomicus* that as far back as his
date, not only hetairæ but married women resorted
to artificial means of beautifying the complexion.

More than one allusion is made in literature to
some kind of hat worn by women ; in Theocritus
(*Idyll*, xv., 39), Praxinoa, when going out to the
festival of Adonis, asks her maid for her wrap and
hat (θολία).

In the *Œdipus Coloneus*[2] Antigone recognises
Ismene from a distance by the Thessalian hat
which she wears as a protection against the heat
of the sun. The words used are κυνῆ Θεσσαλίς, which
seem to imply that the hat was made of some kind
of skin, probably felt, and resembled the men's

[1] Fig. 45 (*k*).   [2] 313.

"petasos," which originated in Thessaly or Thrace ; its shape may have been slightly different. The Tanagra statuettes frequently represent women wearing a broad-brimmed hat with high pointed crown.[1]

[1] Fig. 15.

Fig. ii. Scene from an Attic kylix (ca. 440 B.C.), British Museum. Hartwig, *Meisterschalen*, Pl. 41.

VIII

FOOTGEAR

THE practice of covering the feet seems to have varied somewhat among the Greeks. In all probability it was the custom to go barefoot indoors, and the habit prevailed among certain classes of going always unshod in the street also. It was a mark of hardihood in the Spartan youths always to go barefoot, and at Athens, in addition to the lower orders, who probably never wore shoes, philosophers and those who affected a simple life were in the habit of going unshod. That Socrates rarely covered his feet is proved by more than one reference in Plato's Dialogues ;—Phædrus [1] speaks of him as ἀεί ἀνυπόδητος, "always unshod," and in the *Symposium* [2] we learn that for the occasion of Agathon's banquet Socrates has washed and put on his shoes, ἃ ὀλιγάκις ἐποίει, "which he seldom did."

Other references in literature show that he was not the only philosopher who preferred to have his feet untrammelled. [3]

---

[1] Plato, *Phædrus*, 229 A.   [2] 174 A.
[3] Aristophanes, *The Clouds*, 103 ; Theocritus, XIV., 6.

The normal fashion, however, for people of good breeding was to wear sandals or shoes out of doors, and we learn from Aristophanes[1] that the Athenians at least were particular about the fit;—to "swim about" in large boots was a mark of boorishness. Xenophon[2] notices the division of labour in the shoemakers' trade, where he mentions at least four different hands employed in making a pair of shoes.

The simplest form of footgear was the sandal, the πέδιλον of Homer, the ὑπόδημα of later times; this consisted of a leather sole cut to the shape of the foot and fastened on by means of straps or thongs, passing sometimes round the instep, sometimes between the toes and round the heel and ankle.[3] At times a piece of skin was attached to the sandal at the back, so as to cover the back of the heel, or even to wrap round the instep entirely, leaving only the toes bare;[4] from this form of sandal the ἔμβας, or slipper, was probably developed. This is described by Pollux[5] as εὐτελὲς μὲν ὑπόδημα, Θράκιον δὲ τὸ εὕρημα, "a cheap shoe, of Thracian invention." Its name suffices to show that the foot was inserted into the ἔμβας, in contradistinction to the sandal, which was bound under the foot; and the epithet signifies that it covered the foot completely. This description could be applied to many varieties of shoes and boots represented in extant art. Fig. 46 (e and f) gives two examples of shoes—e being

---

[1] *Knights*, 321.   [2] *Cyropædia*, xviii., 2, 5.
[3] Fig. 46 (a and b); Fig. 48 (c).
[4] Fig. 46 (c and d).   [5] VII., 85.

an ordinary soft shoe covering the foot completely
to the ankle, *f* is turned up at the toes, like a
modern Greek shoe, and reaches above the ankle at
the back. A vase at the British Museum represents
a woman cleaning a shoe of this shape. We learn
from Aristophanes[1] that shoes were cleaned with
blacking made of pitch and applied with a sponge;
they were usually black, except when the leather was
allowed to retain its natural colour. The word
ἔμβας seems to have been used for various kinds of
foot-covering; in Aristophanes it refers sometimes
to a kind of easy slipper worn by old men,[2] and in
other instances it is used of any ordinary shoe or
boot. The mention by Pollux of its Thracian
origin perhaps refers to the high boot turned over
at the top, frequently represented on vase-
paintings as being worn by horsemen with the
Thracian cloak and petasos.[3] Different varieties
of this kind of boot are to be seen in Fig. 46
(*g, h, i,* and *j*).

An article in Daremberg and Saglio's *Dictionnaire* suggests an Asiatic origin, and indeed the
resemblance between Greek boots and those represented on Assyrian monuments is striking. A
comparison is actually made by Herodotus[4] between
Assyrian boots and Bœotian ἐμβάδες.

It is quite possible that boots of this kind may
have come to Greece from the East by way of
Thrace, and the fact that Dionysus is very frequently

---

[1] *The Wasps,* 600.   [2] *The Wasps,* 274; *The Clouds,* 719.
[3] Fig. 22.   [4] I., 195.

represented wearing them seems to add confirmation to this conjecture.

A variety of the ἐμβάδες is to be found in the ἐνδρομίδες, a kind of boot worn by runners, as also by Hermes, Artemis, and the Amazons. They seem to have had no flap at the top, and to have been laced over a tongue either through holes or round buttons.[1] Another kind seems to have consisted of strips of cloth or leather, or possibly felt, wound round the legs like the modern puttees.

FIG. 47.

The word κρηπίδες is frequently used of some kind of foot-covering, and we learn from Theocritus[2] and from Pollux[3] that these were worn by soldiers. The κρῆπις was probably some kind of sandal with a thick sole and stout straps interlacing one another in such a way as to form a protection for the heel and instep.[4] Pliny[5] tells us that sometimes they had nails in them.

Many varieties of shoes or boots are mentioned by Pollux[6] and other ancient writers. We read of ἀρβύλαι, ἀρβυλίδες, a cheap kind of boot worn on journeys ; βλαυταί, light sandals with latchets, called also κονιπόδες, from the fact that they allowed the feet to get covered with dust ; εὐμάριδες, Persian slippers of yellow kid ; Περσικαί, cheap white shoes worn by women, especially by hetairæ ; Λακωνικαί,

---

[1] Figs. 47 and 48 (a).   [2] XV., 6.   [3] VII., 85.
[4] Figs. 48 (b) and 49 (a and b).   [5] XXXV., 25.   [6] VII., 84-93.

distinguished by their red colour — these were probably the same as the 'Αμυκλαί mentioned by Theocritus. One of the archaic female statues in the Acropolis Museum at Athens wears red shoes. Wood was sometimes used for sandals. Pollux

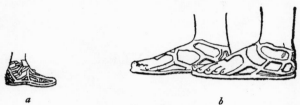

a   *b*

FIG. 49.

tells us that κρουπέζια were a special kind of wooden sandal used for dancing, and that Pheidias represented Athene Parthenos wearing Τυρρηνικά, sandals with high rectangular wooden soles and gold latchets.

Other shoes are too numerous to mention, and cannot be identified with certainty.

IX

THE TOILET

CONCLUSION

THE toilet of the ancient Greeks was quite as elaborate as that of any modern people, and much time and care was bestowed upon it. That of the men was usually performed at the barber's shop (Κουρεῖον), which became, as we gather from frequent allusions in Aristophanes, a regular resort for lounging and picking up news and scraps of gossip of all kinds. A fashionable Athenian would probably spend a whole morning at the barber's shop, where, in addition to having his hair cut and beard clipped or shaved, he could submit to the various operations of manicure and chiropody. An epigram in the palatine anthology[1] gives a list of barber's implements, some of which have survived in a few examples, and may be seen in our museums. The list includes: scissors (ψάλις), razor (ξυρόν), some sharp, pointed instrument for paring and cleaning the nails (στόνυξ). Mention is also made of a scraper (ψήκτρα), which was probably used after bathing.

[1] *Anth. Pal.*, vi., 307.

An ancient razor differs from a modern one, in that it is crescent shaped.

In addition to these implements, various ointments were used, one of which, ψίλωθρον, containing arsenic, was employed for removing superfluous hairs.

FIG. 50.

When repairing to the wrestling school or the gymnasium, a Greek would invariably be provided with an oil-flask (ἀρύβαλλος, λήκυθος) and a strigil (ξύστρα). The aryballos (Fig. 50) was a small globular vessel, with an opening just large enough to allow the oil to trickle slowly out, the lekythos being a long narrow bottle with a foot and a narrow neck.[1] Both were used to carry the olive oil with which athletes were accustomed to anoint themselves. The strigil was a curved metal instrument used for scraping the oil and sand from the body after wrestling. The famous statue of the Apoxyomenos in the Vatican Museum represents an athlete engaged in this operation.

FIG. 51.

The processes and requisites of the feminine toilet were many and various, and toilet scenes are frequently represented in vase-paintings. Sometimes we may see the process of the bath : an attendant slave pouring water from a large vessel over the crouching figure of the bather ; in other

[1] Fig. 51.

instances we find a lady engaged in binding her hair with a fillet, tying her girdle, or fastening her sandal. There is almost invariably a maid in attendance, who assists in the operations, holding a scent-bottle, or a casket from which her mistress selects jewels.[1] One vase-painting shows a lady applying powder or colour to her cheeks with a brush.

Many allusions in literature, and especially in Aristophanes, show that paint and cosmetics of various kinds were in use in Athens in the fifth century B.C. It is not surprising to learn that hetairæ made use of these artificial aids to beauty ; but from a passage in Xenophon's *Œconomicus* [2] we gather that the wives and daughters of respected citizens did not despise such means of enhancing and preserving their appearance. The passage describes how Ischomachus found his young wife ἐντετριμμένην πολλῷ μὲν ψιμυθίῳ ὅπως λευκοτέρα ἔτι δοκοίη εἶναι ἢ ἦν, πόλλῳ δ' ἐγχούσῃ ὅπως ἐρυθροτέρα φαίνοιτο τῆς ἀληθείας, ὑποδήματα δ' ἔχουσαν ὑψηλά, ὅπως μείζων δοκοίη εἶναι ἢ ἐπεφύκει, "with much white lead rubbed into her skin, to make her look fairer than she was ; and with much rouge, to make her appear rosier ; and wearing high sandals, to add to her natural height."

Ischomachus persuades her to give up these vanities, asking her if she will like him better if he goes about μίλτῳ ἀλειφόμενος καὶ τοὺς ὀφθαλμοὺς ὑπαλειφόμενος, "anointed with red ochre, and with pigment under his eyes."

[1] Fig. 52 (a). [2] x., 2.

White lead was commonly used for producing a
fair complexion ; it was prepared by laying lead in
vinegar, scraping off, powdering, and heating the
white rust thus formed.[1] Various substances were
used for producing rouge—some mineral, some
vegetable ; of the latter, the root of a plant (ἔγχουσα
or ἄγχουσα), certain kinds of seaweed (φῦκος), and
mulberry juice (συκάμινον), were common. That some
kind of pigment was used for darkening the eyelids
is further testified by Pollux[2] and Aristophanes.[3]
Lamp-black and a sulphuret of antimony (στίμμις),
were used for blackening eyebrows and eyelids.
Perfumed powders and unguents were used for skin
and hair, scented with myrrh or roses or other
products. The simplest and most common unguent
was, of course, olive oil. In addition to artificial
complexions, we learn that false hair and wigs
(πηνίκη, προκομίον), were not unknown, and that these
came from the East.[4]

Many examples have survived of the various
articles pertaining to the equipment of a Greek
lady's toilet-table. Combs, hair-pins, mirrors,
boxes, and bottles are numerous in our museums.
Combs are usually made of ivory or bone, with a
double row of rather fine teeth. Hair-pins of bone,
ivory, or metal consist of a single pin with an
ornamental head. Mirrors are of highly polished
metal, usually bronze, though some have been
found in silver. The mirrors may be divided into

---

[1] *Theophr. de Lapidibus*, 56.   [2] VII., 95   [3] Fragment 695.
[4] See Xenophon's *Cyropædeia*, I., iii., 2.

two classes—disk-mirrors and box-mirrors. The former consists of a single disk polished on one side, the reverse being usually engraved. The disk is furnished with a handle, which is sometimes so constructed that it can serve also as a foot; the mirror can so be made to stand on a table. The handle of a mirror of this kind very frequently takes the form of a human figure.[1] The box-mirror consists of two disks, the lower one, with its polished upper surface, serving as the mirror, the upper one as a cover to protect it. The two are sometimes quite separate and fit closely on to one another, but more often they are joined by a hinge; the cover is usually ornamented with relief work, a favourite subject being Aphrodite and Eros, although other mythological scenes are also found.[2]

Of the various receptacles used for containing trinkets, hair-bands, cosmetics, and so on, the commonest is the pyxis, although we find also baskets and little square caskets represented in vase-paintings and on the Attic grave reliefs. A box for cosmetics in the British Museum is in the shape of a bird.[3] The pyxis is a circular box with a lid; its sides are sometimes straight, but more often concave, and it is frequently raised on a foot. Its material was originally boxwood, hence its name, πύξις; but the majority of those which are extant are terra-cotta, though they are known also in ivory, alabaster, and precious metals. A common

[1] Fig. 53 (b).   [2] Fig. 53 (a).   [3] Fig. 52 (b).

subject on a terra-cotta pyxis is a toilet scene or a marriage procession.[1]

The alabastron used to contain unguents or perfumes is a long narrow bottle with a spreading neck and small opening; it has no foot, and is round at the bottom, so that some kind of stand must have been necessary to hold it upright when not in use.[2] It was usually made of stone, alabaster, or terra-cotta. The lekythos also was sometimes used for the same purpose.

That Greek ladies wore abundant jewellery is proved by frequent representations both in sculpture and vase-paintings, as also by actual finds of jewellery, notably in the Greek graves of the fourth century at Kertch. These objects have been described and discussed by Mr A. B. Walters, in his book on *The Art of the Greeks*.[3] Rings, bracelets, necklaces, brooches, and ear-rings, were commonly worn, as well as orna-mental hair-pins and metal diadems for the hair. Many examples of goldsmith's work are extant including some gold ornaments set with precious stones.

FIG. 54.

In summing up the results of the foregoing enquiry, we find that the nature and development of the costume of the Greeks is entirely in accord-ance with what we know of the nature and development of the national character. The chief

[1] Fig. 52 (*a*).   [2] Fig. 54.   [3] Page 259 ff.

characteristics of the Doric dress, which was probably worn in early days by all the inhabitants of the mainland alike, is a certain broad simplicity; that of the Ionic dress, which was worn by the Asiatic Greeks, and for a short period at least by the Athenians also, is graceful elegance. These characteristics distinguish the Doric and Ionic temperaments as exhibited in art also, notably in architecture, and to some extent also in sculpture. Athens appears to have occupied a middle position between the Peloponnese and Ionia. The Peloponnesians seem to have clung throughout their history to the Dorian dress, as the Ionians probably did to the Ionic; but in Athens we find change and development most strongly marked. In very early days the Athenians wore the Doric dress; then in the course of the seventh and sixth centuries their intercourse with the East brought them into contact with Eastern ideas and Eastern customs, and they appear to have caught something of the luxury which was characteristic of the East. At any rate, for a time at least they adopted the Ionic dress, and carried it to a great degree of luxury and extravagance. Then with the Persian wars came a reaction against anything savouring of Orientalism, and a return to greater simplicity. This led to a resumption of the Doric dress, with certain modifications and the retention of some Ionic elements.

It can hardly be questioned that the freedom and simplicity of their dress was to a great extent the cause of the development of the splendid physique which the Greeks undoubtedly enjoyed. Their loose draperies allowed their limbs perfect freedom, and their bodies were unhampered by constraint of any kind.   In the palæstra and the gymnasium, air and sunlight were allowed to exercise their salutary influence, for the Greeks were not "ashamed of their own naked skin," and so discarded their clothing when in pursuit of their athletic occupations.   The healthy state of body thus preserved no doubt had its share in fostering that healthy state of mind to which are due the sanity and sobriety that characterise all Greek thought, whether expressed in literature, art, or philosophy.

Fig. iii. Detail from scene on red-figured pyxis (toilet box). (ca. 470 B.C.) British Museum. Sleeveless Dorian chiton.

ENGLISH INDEX

R

GREEK INDEX

PLATE CC

Fig. iv. Black-figured Attic lekythos (ca. 550 B.C.) New York
Metropolitan Museum of Art. Women weaving cloth.

PLATE DD

Fig. v. Black-figured Attic neck-amphora (ca. 540 B.C.) New

Fig. vi. Black-figured Attic amphora (ca. 540 B.C.) New York Metropolitan Museum of Art. Maidens in Attic chitons of mid-sixth c. B.C. and nude youths watching the hero

Fig. vii. Red-figured Attic amphora (ca. 490 B.C.) New York Metropolitan Museum of Art. Youth wearing long Ionian chiton with himation over his shoulders, singing and playing the lyre.

Fig. viii. Black figured oinochoe (wine jar) (ca. 550 B.C.) Chicago Natural History Museum. Young girls wearing long chitons playing the lyre and singing.

Fig. ix. a) White lekythos (ca. 410 B.C.) Chicago Natural History Museum. b) Drawing of the painting by Susan

Fig. x. White Attic lekythos (ca. 410 B.C.) Chicago Natural History Museum. Old woman wearing long chiton and

Fig. xii. Red-figured pelike (ca. 350 B.C.) Chicago Natural History Museum. Scene of water divination by winged genius. Woman wears sphendone (hair support), lorfg chiton fastened at shoulders and folded himation.

Fig. xi. Detail of red-figured Campanian bell amphora (ca. 360 B.C.) Chicago Natural History Museum. Prophetess wearing long chiton fastened at shoulders and on rock; youth brings divination bowl.

Fig. xiii. Red-figured Attic bell krater (ca. 440 B.C.) New York Metropolitan Museum of Art. Orpheus playing the lyre for a Thracian chief who wears short rider's chiton. heavy himation, folded down leather greaves and the typical Thracian hood. Woman approaching with sickle in left hand wears long chiton fastened at shoulders and a sphendone in her hair.

Fig. xiv. White Attic pyxis with lid (ca. 465-460 B.C.) New York Metropolitan Museum of Art. Paris, seated, wears short chiton and petassos (hat). Hermes wears heavy himation. Hera wears a peplos (veil), tiara with veil, long Ionian chiton and heavily embroidered himation.

Fig. xv. Red-figured Attic oinochoe (ca. 465 B.C.) New York Metropolitan Museum of Art. Youth running with hoop and game cock. Chiton heavily embroidered at hem.

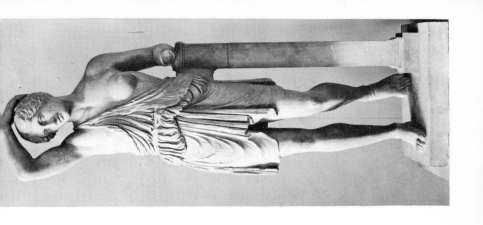

Fig. xvi. Red-figured Italiotic krater (ca. 340 B.C.) Chicago
Natural History Museum. Young horseman wearing short
Tracian rider's chiton with wide belt.

Fig. xvii. Bronze statuette of Mithradates VI Eupator (ca.
87 B.C.) British Museum. Short Thracian rider's chiton,
wide belt and lion helmet and skin worn rather than a
himation.

Fig. xviii. The Polykleitan Amazon. New York Metropolitan
Museum of Art. Roman copy of Greek original (ca.
440-430 B.C.) showing short chiton.

xix.

xx.

xxi.

xxii.

Fig. xix. Roman copy of Eirene by Kephisodotos (ca. 375-370 B.C.) New York Metropolitan Museum of Art. Dorian chiton.

Fig. xx. Sandal-binder. Relief from Nike Temple parapet. Athens, Acropolis Museum. Woman's long Ionian chiton (ca. 410-407 B.C.)

Fig. xxi. Apollo by Euphranor (ca. 350-330 B.C.) Athens, Agora Museum. Man's long Ionian chiton.

Fig. xxii. Athena Medici (ca. 430 B.C.) Paris, Louvre, Long Attic Ionian chiton.

CHAPTERS

ON

GREEK DRESS

BY

MARIA MILLINGTON EVANS

Fig. 6.—Women at a Fountain. From a Vase Painting, British Museum.

Fig. xxiii. Black-figured hydria (ca. 520 B.C.) Boston Museum
of Fine Arts. Women at fountain-house.

CONTENTS.

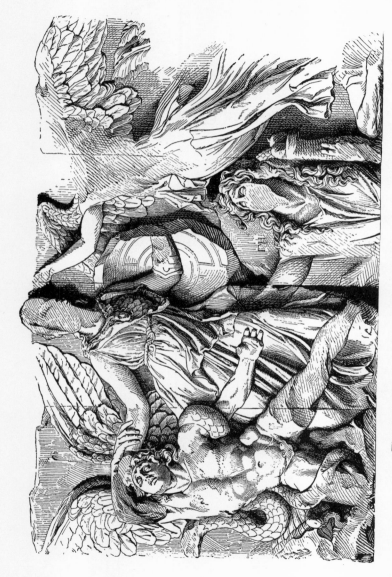

Fig. 53.—Athena. Slab from the Great Altar, Pergamos. Berlin.

LIST OF ILLUSTRATIONS.

LIST OF ILLUSTRATIONS.

Fig. 50.—Boys at School. Vase signed by Duris. Berlin.

INTRODUCTION.

In attempting to give a sketch of the main principles
on which the ordinary dress of the ancient Greeks was
based, I do not propose to deal with the subject in an
exhaustive manner, nor do I for a moment pretend that the
materials used are entirely original. But, having noticed
in pictures of classical scenes and in Greek costume when
exhibited on the stage, some ignorance of the elements
of the subject, I venture to make public the following
pages in the hope that they may be of service to those
who, from archæological or artistic causes, wish to obtain
a correct insight into the character of the Greek dress in
classical times. In the desire to make the national col-
lections as useful as possible, I have made frequent
reference to examples in the British Museum, Blooms-
bury, or in the collection of casts at the South Kensington
Museum.

My debt to the labours of others, specially of German
archæologists, is great. To Dr. Studniczka I tender my
best thanks for permission to reproduce many illustrations
from his work. My thanks are also due to Messrs.
Murray, Macmillan, and Swan Sonnenschein, as well as to
the trustees of the British Museum for the loan of woodcuts.
The sources of the illustrations are acknowledged in the

list at p. ix. My friend Professor Gardner, of Oxford, has added to his many kindnesses that of reading my proofs.

I subjoin a list of works consulted that may be of use to other students of the subject.

"Beiträge zur Geschichte der Altgriechischen Tracht," von Franz Studniczka. Karl Gerold's Sohn. Wien, 1886.
"Quaestiones de re Vestiaria Graecorum." J. Boehlau. Weimar. 1884.
"Quaestiones Vestiariae." W. Müller. Göttingen, 1890.
"Lehrbuch der Griechischen Privatalterthümer." Hermann. Dritte Auflage von H. Blumner. (Band iv. of Hermann's Lehrbuch der Griech. Antiquitäten.) J. C. B. Mohr. Freiburg, 1882.
"Die Tracht bei Homer." Friederich. "Realien" (p. 248 and foll.), zweite Ausgabe. F. Enke. Erlangen, 1856.
"Das Homerische Epos." Helbig. Leipzig, 1884.
"Social Life in Greece." J. P. Mahaffy. 5th edition. Macmillan. London, 1888.
"Journal of Hellenic Studies," vol. viii., p. 170. E. Gardner. 1887. Published for the Society for Promoting Hellenic Studies, by Macmillan & Co.
"Histoire de la Sculpture Grecque." Maxime Collignon. Paris, 1882.
"A Companion to the Iliad." Walter Leaf. Macmillan. 1892.
"Olympia," "Bronzen." A. Furtwaengler. Taf. xxi. and foll. (Band iv. of "Olympia," herausgegeben von E. Curtius und F. Adler). A. Asher. Berlin, 1890.
Hope's "Costume of the Ancients." London, 1812.
Articles on special garments in Daremberg and Saglio's "Dictionnaire des Antiquités Grecques et Romaines." Hachette & Co., Paris (still in progress).
Similar articles in Baumeister's "Denkmäler des Klassischen Altertums." Munich and Leipzig, 1885, etc.
Articles in the "Jahrbuch des Kais. Inst." Berlin, 1892. vii. 4., by Mayer, and 1891, vii. 1., by Hauser.

" Observations sur les statues archaïques de type féminin du Musée de l'Acropole." H. Lechat in the " Bulletin de Correspond. Hellénique," 1890.

" Die Griechischen Meisterschalen," by Paul Hartwig. Published by Spemann, Stuttgart and Berlin, 1893.

The following table of the periods of Greek Art is given for convenience of reference :—

I. Prehistoric (Mycenae, Tiryns, &c.). To about 700 B.C.
II. Archaic. (Artists as Antenor, Calamis, &c.) *Circa* 700 to 460 B.C. Period of the Vases with Black Figures.
III. Early Fine Art. (Sculptures of Temple of Olympia, Parthenon, &c.) *Circa* 460 to 400 B.C. Period of the earlier vases with Red Figures.
IV. Late Fine Art. (Artists of the Mausoleum, Praxiteles, Scopas, &c.) *Circa* 400 to 300 B.C. Period of the later vases with Red Figures.
V. Decline. (Artists of Pergamene sculptures, &c.) *Circa* 300 to 100 B.C. Period of the vases of Apulia and Campania.

Maria Millington Evans.

Nash Mills,
Hemel Hempstead,

Fig. xxiv. Detail from black-figured painting from vase at Florence.

Fig. 54.—Fragment of a robe. Crimea.

Fig. 44.—Sophocles. Lateran, Rome.

GREEK DRESS.

I.

HOMERIC DRESS.

To some persons it may seem a trivial undertaking to set to work to describe the garments worn by a people so far removed in time from our own day as the ancient Greeks. But though removed in time, there is no race whose spirit is more vitally present as an influence in modern thought. True, that the spirit of a great past can be caught without technical accuracy as to its dress —as witness the fact that Mrs. Siddons, in an ordinary ball-dress of the period, could so play the part of Shakspeare's heroines as to make spectators forget the anachronism of her clothes. But there can be little doubt that a clearer idea of ancient life is obtained if we can picture the people "in their habit as they lived." To use the words of quaint old Hope,[1] "To clothe, as Paul Veronese has done, Alexander in French brocade and Statira in Genoa cut velvet, is beforehand wantonly to mar the best fruits of one's labour, the applause of the judicious. It is offering a masquerade instead of a historic subject, a riddle in place of a tale clearly told."

But the subject is not without its difficulties. It is

[1] *Costume of the Ancients*, 1812.

B

easy to speak of the " Greeks," but Greece was at no
period a uniform whole, with customs common to every
part of it. No two towns could have been more dis-
similar in habits and thought than Sparta, where everything was subservient to the military ideal, and Athens
with her " grace without softness." How great, even,
were the differences between Corinth the commercial and
Thebes the prosperous, and those more distant centres,
Miletus, Cyrene, Syracuse, each tinged by influences of
their surroundings!

The sources of information, too, are not quite so numerous as those available for other branches of ancient history.
For example — inscriptions, usually such sure guides
in Greek matters, throw but little light on the subject,
though certainly one list of the temple treasures at Samos
gives the wardrobe of the image of Hera,[2] a list almost as
long as the inventory of the ornaments and apparel of a
mediæval abbey, or as that of the clothes left by Queen
Elizabeth. Other lists of garments dedicated in temples
also occur.

But the sources readily available for our inquiry are
mainly two, viz..:—

1. The literary, *i.e.* mention of garments, in Greek
literature, and especially the express statements of some
ancient Greek historians on the subject.

2. The artistic, by far the larger class, *i.e.* garments as
shown in ancient Greek sculpture, terra-cottas and vase-
paintings. But here some allowance has constantly to be
made either for the personal vagaries of the artist, or for
the limitations of his art.

[2] Curtius *Urkunde und Studien;* "Samos," p. 15; Taf.,
15—16.

In the case of dress in Homer, it is difficult to conclude by the light of existing monuments how far the state of culture represented in the poems actually existed, how much of what is described was a setting of past and present realities tinged by the glamour of poetry, and in the case of monuments, how long forms were retained in art after they had fallen out of daily use.

Thus much, however, may be safely inferred from the Homeric writings. Garments (εἵματα, ἐσθής) are woven by the lady of the house and her maidens.[3] Athena, the patron of the arts among the gods, does not disdain such womanly pursuits. Among mortals the Phœnicians are conspicuous. The finest robes in the Trojan king's treasure are the "work of Sidonian women."[4] Woven garment-stuffs in Homer are stored in large quantity. They form part of the treasure (κειμήλια) of a house. When the body of Hector is ransomed from Achilles, robes are part of the price paid. They are favourite offerings to the gods.[5] These robes were each woven as one garment, separate and complete in itself. There was no weaving of a long piece of stuff from which a length could be cut as required, a method with which we are nowadays so familiar. Such commercial convenience was alien to the Greek idea of simple fitness and completeness.

These woven materials are stated to have been of wool.[6] There is no special record of the working of flax in Homer, but yet linen (λίνον) is mentioned, as in the case

---

[3] *Iliad*, iii., 388 ; *Od.*, xviii., 316 ; *Iliad*, xxii., 511, &c.
[4] *Iliad*, vi., 289.
[5] *Cf. Iliad*, xxiv., 229, VI., 90, 271.
[6] *Iliad*, xvi., 224 ; *Od.*, iv., 50, 135, &c.

of bed-clothes,[7] a linen corslet,[8] a fishing-line,[9] and fishing nets[10] of flaxen twine. The thread of the Fates was of flax.[11] From this frequent mention of flax it has been conjectured that linen cloth was a home production of Greece in Homer's time, though it may have been imported from the East, or the thread may have been imported and woven in Greece by the women. Linen was known in the East at a very early period, and even in classical Roman times the wearing of linen garments was considered a sign of oriental effeminacy. In those days Cos was the centre of a manufacture of transparent garments, as may be gathered from the mention of "Coae vestes" by Tibullus and Propertius.

With regard to the dress of the men in Homer, the chiton (χιτών) played an important part, but the text gives no precise information as to its material or form, though its appearance is denoted by various epithets, as "shining," "soft," and the like.[12] By all accounts it seems to have been a sewn, shirt-like garment, not fastened with fibulae or pins, and probably made of linen, as its brilliancy is insisted upon.[13] In the representations of the human figure on some of the gems, vases, and other relics belonging to the prehistoric period of Greece, the men wear a kind of bathing-drawers or short double apron (cf. the "Man and Bull" wall-painting from Tiryns[14] and the gold cups from Vapheio[15]). In

---

[7] Iliad, ix., 661.　　　[8] Iliad, ii., 529.　　　[9] Iliad, xvi., 408.

[10] Iliad, v., 487.　　　[11] Iliad, xx., 128; Od., vii., 198.

[12] Iliad, ii., 42, &c.　　　[13] Cf. Iliad, xviii., 595.

[14] Given in Schuchhardt's Schliemann's Excavations. English translation by E. Sellers. Macmillan, 1891, p. 120.

[15] Schuchhardt, op. cit. p. 350; cf. Dr. Leaf's Introductory chapter to that same work, pp. xxvii.—xxix.

Greek art of what is known as the early "archaic" period, the short chiton sits closely, jersey-fashion, to the skin. On later archaic Greek monuments the short chiton worn under armour is fuller and falls in folds (*cf.* Warrior of west pediment of Temple of Aegina, cast in British Museum, Archaic Room, 160). The length of the Homeric chiton does not seem to have been uniform in all cases. That worn by Odysseus as a beggar (Od., xiii., 434; xix., 450) must have only reached to the knee, or else the scar would not have been visible, but some passages[15a] may be taken to imply that, at least in the case of elder and more venerable wearers and the "Ionians," it was longer; and this is borne out by the evidence of archaic monuments, where the long chiton falls to the feet. (Fig. 1, *a, b, c.*)

The ordinary daily dress of middle-aged men in Homer, when engaged in active pursuits, such as war or hunting, seems to have been a kind of jerkin, perhaps of felt or leather, worn under the harness to prevent friction to the skin, and to promote general comfort (*cf.* British Museum, "Euphorbos pinax," 1st Vase Room, Case D, No. A 268). This dress is evidently short. When Menelaos is wounded in the side, the blood runs down over his legs, implying that these are bare. Sometimes, even, the word "chiton," instead of being used for the jerkin, designates the actual coat of mail. Idomeneus wounds Alcathoos through his χιτῶνα χάλκεον,[16] but the word is not generally used in this sense.

As we now find it represented on early black-figured

[15a] *Iliad*, v., 734—736, but *cf.* W. Müller: "Quaestiones Vestiariae," p. 1; xiii., 685; *Od.*, xix., 242.

[16] *Iliad*, xiii., 439.

vases made in Greece (for example, in the instances in the
British Museum, Vase-room II., No. B. 53, pedestal 1 ;
pub. in Miss Harrison's *Myths and Monuments*, p. 432)

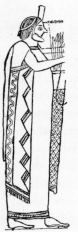

Fig. 1 (*a*).—Peleus,   Fig. 1 (*b*).—From a   Fig. 1 (*c*). —From a
from a Vase Painting.   Vase Painting.   Vase Painting.

and as shown in Fig. 1, the long Homeric chiton of
peace is ungirdled.   This custom of wearing the long
chiton was retained for all " cultus " garments of classical
Greece, that is for garments worn on solemn and religious

occasions; for example, in representations of Apollo playing the lyre ("Citharoedus") as in Fig. 1 *b*, or in the well-
known statue of this god in the Vatican (Fig. 2), or in the
figure of the priest of the east frieze of the Parthenon
(British Museum, Elgin Room, Slab No. V., Fig. 33).

For ordinary informal dress
in the house in Homeric times
the woven chiton, long or
short, seems to have been worn
alone. Out of doors a cloak
(χλαῖνα), apparently an early
variety of the later himation
(ἱμάτιον), made of wool and
dyed in colours, was put on
scarf fashion or like a shawl
folded lengthwise (Fig. 1,
a, b). Being evidently rather
long and cumbrous it is thrown
off to increase facilities of
speed. Odysseus tells how it
is discarded for convenience
in moving actively among the
men.[17] Telemachos,[18] when
about to make trial of the

Fig. 2.—Apollo Citharoedus.
Vatican.

bow, "rising, puts off from his shoulder his purple cloak."

As an outer covering the skins of animals were worn
in Homeric times. Agamemnon,[19] Diomedes,[20] Menelaos[21] wear the skins of lions and leopards. Representations of such skins, with the paws of the animal hanging

---

[17] *Od.*, xiv., 500.   [18] *Od.*, xxi., 118.

[19] *Iliad*, x., 23.   [20] *Iliad*, x., 177.

[21] *Iliad*, x., 29.

down as a finish in front, are not at all rare on some early
Greek vases (Fig. 3), where Heracles, Meleager, Iris, and
Hermes all wear them. In the country men wear goat
skins.[22] Pan, as a country god in the Homeric hymn
(19, 23), wears on his shoulders the pelt
of a spotted lynx.

Fig. 3.—Hermes.
From the François
Vase, Florence.

The dress of the women in Homer
consists chiefly of the " Peplos," *i.e.* an
under-garment which probably reached
to the feet and sometimes trailed behind,
worn with a girdle. The word "peplos"
is one that occurs in the Greek tragedians
also, but by them it is not used in quite
the same sense as by Homer. Thus
Aeschylus uses it both of men's and
women's dress.[23] In fact, in the tragedians the words πέπλος, πέπλωμα seem to be the general
poetic term for "garment." The "peplos" in Homer
may be taken as the equivalent of that dress known in
later times as the "Dorian" chiton, the typical classical
dress of Greece, of which I shall have a good deal to say
later. It is distinguished from the chiton of the men
by the fact that, whereas theirs is a sewn garment put
on like a shirt, the women's peplos is a piece of cloth
merely fastened with pins. The peplos presented by
Antinoos to Penelope had twelve such pins (περόναι).[24]
The garment was all of one piece, and was probably left
open at one side like the dress of the Dorian maidens
that I shall subsequently describe. When Aphrodite

---

[22] *Od.*, xiv., 530.
[23] *Persae*, 468, 1031; *Cf. Soph. Trach.*, 602; and *Eur.
Hec.*, 465—473.   [24] *Od.*, xviii., 292.

would protect her son Aineias, she flings open her peplos
and veils him in its shining folds as a protection against
the darts.[25] The most frequent epithet applied to women
in Homer is " white-armed " (λευκώλενος), which implies
the absence of a sleeve. This was also a characteristic of
the true Dorian chiton, which originally seems to have
been without sleeves and therefore distinct from the dress
of the Easterns.

The stuff of the Homeric peplos is never expressly
mentioned. Its colour is spoken of as " variegated "
(ποικίλος),[26] and it is described as μαλακός, soft, and
λεπτός,[27] thin or fine. Hence it may, in some degree,
have resembled our Indian shawls.

For an over-dress, a veil-like piece of stuff, the " Kre-
demnon" (κρήδεμνον), or " Kaluptre " (καλύπτρη), is worn
by ladies in Homer ;[28] Penelope and other ladies of high
degree are mentioned as wearing it. The maidens of
Nausicaa lay it aside. Perhaps it may have been an addition worn by women of rank. The mourning Thetis[29] when
preparing to go to Olympus wears a dark-coloured veil,
but it seems that only in the direst grief was the coun-
tenance completely covered. The veils in Homer are
spoken of as white and shining, and may probably have
been linen, inasmuch as wool would have been too heavy.
The veil of Hera[30] is compared to the sun for brilliancy, a
simile that would hardly be applied to the dead surface of
wool, and evidence for silk in Homeric times is hardly
forthcoming. Many pieces of small, generally folded,
drapery occur in the Homeric descriptions, such as the

[25] *Iliad*, v., 315.   [26] *Iliad*, v., 735.
[27] *Od.*, vii., 97.   [28] *Od.*, i., 334.
[29] *Iliad*, xxiv., 94.   [30] *Iliad*, xiv., 185.

"lope" ($\lambda\acute{\omega}\pi\eta$)[31] and others, as well as those I have mentioned, but I will not linger over a detailed consideration of them.

It is not easy to reconcile the account given in Homer with the very earliest prehistoric representations of women's dress found in Greece, though a fairly close parallel may be established between the decorations of early black-figured vases and the Homeric account.

Fig. 4 (*a*).—Gold Seal from Mycenae.　Twice linear measure.

On the gold seal from Mycenae (Fig. 4, *a*) the women seem to wear an extremely tight-fitting bodice and a frilled or tucked skirt.　These frills may represent the dress of the period, or the gem may be of foreign workmanship denoting foreign, probably oriental, styles of dress.　A curious parallel is found in the dress of the Rutenu women of Egyptian wall-paintings (Fig. 4, *b*). A similar dress seems to be represented in a wall-picture

[31] *Od.*, xiii., 224.

from the group of buildings on the south wall,[32] Mycenae, and on the gem from Vapheio (Fig. 4, c).[32a] It may, perhaps, be assumed that the inhabitants of Greece at the period represented by the tombs of the " shaft " form at Mycenae, wore a somewhat similar dress, though the pin, one of the necessities of the Doric chiton, has been found there. In the tombs outside the citadel, fibulae of the " safety-pin " form have lately been discovered.

Some authorities (as Studniczka and Müller) find that

Fig. 4 (b).—Rutenu Woman.

Fig. 4 (c).—Gem from Vapheio.
Twice linear measure.

the Homeric peplos is pretty much the same as the women's dress on the François vase in the Etruscan Museum at Florence, a piece of painting that may be referred to about B.C. 550 or earlier, some figures from which are given in Fig. 5. On other early black-figured vases also the women's garments frequently agree very closely in detail with the Homeric description. They generally show the straight chiton, shorter or longer as may be, sometimes with a girdle, sometimes without, but frequently of so narrow a

[32] Figured in Schuchhardt, op. cit. p. 291, fig. 288.
[32a] Cf. Ἐφημερὶς Ἀρχαιολογική, 1889, pl. x., 34.

shape that walking comfortably in such garments would have been out of the question. This excessive narrowness can hardly have existed as a fact, but must be set down as in a great measure due to the limitations of early art and the difficulty it experienced in the adequate repre-

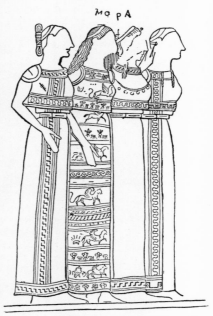

Fig. 5.—Moirae. From the François Vase, Florence.

sentation of falling folds. Instances of such garments are given in Fig. 6. For further instances of them the reader is referred to the British Museum, 2nd Vase Room, Nos. B 333, Case 45, or B 379, Case H.

Down the front of these garments broad bands of decoration are frequently found. Some writers think

that these served as an edging to an actual opening
down the front, or were, at any rate, a survival from an
opening that once existed and was so trimmed. But it
is a well-known fact in archaic art that, like a child
attempting to depict the human figure, the early artist
loves to represent the upper part of the body full-face,

Fig. 7.—From an archaic Terra Cotta. Santangelo Collection,
Naples Museum.

and the lower in profile, and *vice versâ*. It has been suggested by Helbig that to this custom the stripe down the
centre of either the body or skirt drapery may be referred,
being derived from an opening that really ran down the
side of the wearer—a characteristic in the Laconian-
Dorian chiton—a pattern of which I propose to give
later. In archaic black-figured vases, as in Figs. 5 and

6, it is usual to find the surface of the dresses covered with minute, elaborately scratched patterns. An instance of a richly-decorated robe is given in Fig. 7, where a "choros" of dancing men and maidens and a Homeric subject (?) are represented on the stiff foldless surface of a dress. Occasionally, as I shall subsequently have to insist, these patterns on dresses in Greek Art vary suddenly on the same surface, and it is not unreasonable to suppose that the artist, wishing to make his work as pretty as possible, may have been moved to add a band of decoration here and there regardless of the actual make of the garment. Or, such bands of embroidery may have been imported from the East and sewn on as a trimming by the Greeks, in similar fashion to the "orphreys" on copes and chasubles in mediæval days. But it is time to return to the Homeric description.

From what I have said I hope it is clear that the main divisions of dress in Homeric time, were broadly *two*, both for men and women, viz. :

    1. The class of " endymata " ('ενδυμάτα), *i.e.* garments worn near or next the skin.

    2. The class of " epiblemata " (ἐπιβλήματα), *i.e.* mantles of various cut thrown over these in shawl or veil fashion as a suitably modest out-of-doors dress and a protection against the weather.

These two classes of garments prevailed also in historic Greek times, both for men and women. For men two garments were generally sufficient. In the case of women these two were often supplemented by two or three others. This may easily be seen in the course of a walk round the galleries of the British Museum or the Cast Collection at South Kensington.

II.

DRESS IN HISTORIC GREECE.

UNDER-GARMENTS OF THE WOMEN.

I NOW propose to enter more in detail into the two classes of garments, the "endymata," or garments worn next the skin, and the "epiblemata," or wraps thrown over these, which prevailed in Historic as they seem to have done in Homeric times. Dates in such matters are exceedingly difficult to give. They have rather to be extracted from the evidence than laid down in any arbitrary fashion. For instance, the date assigned for the commencement of the "Historic" period in Greek history has changed a good deal even since Grote's day, and is still ever liable to be shifted in consequence of fresh results from the excavator's spade. But I will endeavour to give a few "milestone" dates, leaving the rest to the reader's own industry.

Taking first the class of "endymata" to which the generic name of "chiton" ($\chi\iota\tau\acute{\omega}\nu$) may be given. The origin of the dress is not to be affirmed with certainty. The word used ($\chi\iota\tau\acute{\omega}\nu$ = Kuttonet, Kethoneth (Heb.), and Kittûn (Chald.), as given by Dr. Studniczka (p. 15, op. cit.), seems to point to an oriental source. The short chiton, according to Dr. Müller (p. 8, op. cit.), is found among the peoples in Asia Minor before the ascendency of the kingdoms of Lydia and Persia. In a slightly longer form it is found among the Egyptians. From the East this garment may have made its way into Greece through Phœnician agency. It is mentioned in Homer as an accepted and ordinary garment for the "Ionians," and may have come into Greece from the ancient inhabitants of Asia Minor. From the fact that the chiton is not found, so far as is at present known, on the monuments of prehistoric art at Mycenae and other centres, it can hardly be supposed that it was, in the very earliest times, known to the Greeks in Greece. The Asiatic peoples mentioned above may (I again cite Dr. Müller) have obtained it from Babylon, for the short chiton appears on some of their very oldest rock-sculptures as having been worn by the Babylonians.

The long tunic or chiton seems to have come into Greece later than the short, though it occurs in the East among very much the same people, viz., the Chaldæans and the Assyrians.[33]

Dr. Müller assumes that the long chiton probably passed from Assyria to the Phœnicians, thence to the coast of the Asiatic side of the Ægean, and so to Greece itself. After the age of Homer the Greeks seem, except for wear on solemn and religious occasions, to have preferred the short woollen tunic to the long linen one.

The following is a description of the Dorian or long woollen chiton of the women, the χιτὼν ποδήρης, which in the main seems to correspond with the peplos of Homer, together with what appears to have been the ancient method of arranging it :—

[33] *Cf. Hdt.*, I., 195.

A large piece of material is chosen, A B C D (*cf.* Fig. 8), in the direction A D and B C about a foot longer than the extreme height of the figure of the wearer, and in the. direction B A and C D as long as the distance from tip to tip of the hands with the arms stretched out to their widest extent. This piece is then taken, and the upper edge of it folded over (ἀπότυγμα, apotygma) about the depth of from the neck to the waist, A E, B F, of the diagram. Then the whole piece is doubled at G H, and the lengths F G, E G, are divided into three. It is generally supposed that these were three equal parts, but it is found in practice that this leaves too much for the neck, and that when a garment so divided is put on it immediately falls off again. This difficulty seems to have been felt by the Greeks, and at a later period (about 200—168 B.C.) some-

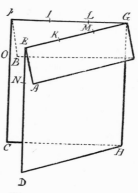

Fig. 8.—Scheme of the Dorian Chiton.

thing very like " gathers " is found on the monuments in this part of the dress, and even then it seems slipping off! (Fig. 9.) At the finest period a pleated fold occurs in the front of the neck, *i.e.* in the middle section K M, I L (Fig. 10), but how this was produced is not very clear. It may have been secured by pinning.

The points I L and K M being taken, the garment is folded round the body ; these points are made to corre- spond, and are fastened on the shoulder by means of pins (Fig. 11).

Thus one gets one side of the person covered by the

closed side G H, and the side A E D and B F C remains open.

Epithets, such as φαικομηρίς ("showing the thigh"), used of Laconian maidens, imply that this

Fig. 11.—Dress fastened on the Shoulder. From a Vase Painting.

side was so left open among them,[34] and instances of this custom are found in Art (Figs. 12, 13). The

"Iris" of the Parthenon Pediment (British Museum,

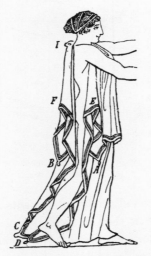
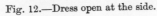

Fig. 12.—Dress open at the side.

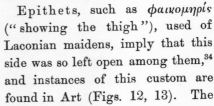

Fig. 13.—Dress open at the side.

Elgin Room, No. G) and the woman in the group from the Temple at Bassae (British Museum, Phigaleia Room, No. 524) wear chitons open at the side.

[34] *Cf. Eur. Androm.* 598, and *Hec.* 933. *Cf.* also Müller's *Dorians*, iv., 2, 3.

But in practice this seems to have been generally modified. The open side was closed by some means (either sewing or pins), partially, at D N, C O (see Fig. 8), or wholly (Figs. 14, 15).

After putting on the chiton, the wearer of the garment stands up, with extended arms, and a girdle is passed round the waist by some one standing behind, and the superfluous length is pulled up through the girdle, and allowed to hang over it in a kind of bag, the κόλπος, "kolpos" (Fig. 15). To this class of the wholly or partially closed Dorian chiton belongs the dress of the maidens of the Parthenon frieze (British Museum, Elgin Room, No. 324, Slabs VII., VIII., Figs. 52 — 60), the Caryatid of the Erechtheum porch (same room, No. 407), the bronzes from Hercula- neum, now in the Naples

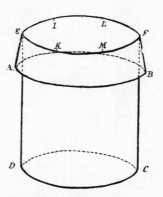

Fig. 14.—Scheme of the closed Dorian Chiton.

Museum (Figs. 16, 17), and the metope from the Temple of Zeus, Olympia (Fig. 18), of which a cast may be seen in the South Kensington collection. (Perry's Catalogue, No. 78e.)

Sometimes the piece of the apotygma falling down the back is drawn over the head as a veil. The girl, in Fig. 17, seems about to draw hers up.

Another way of dealing with the large square of material is to omit the folding over of A E, B F, and to take points parallel to I L, K M, in the upper edge of the unfolded stuff, thus having no apotygma, and then to draw the whole superfluous length through the girdle (*cf.*

Fig. 15.—Girl wearing the closed Dorian Chiton.

Fig. 16.—Girl putting on partially closed Dorian Chiton. Naples Museum.

the figure with the child in Fig. 19). Or the piece folded over at A E, B F, may be made so deep that no girdle is required, since there is nothing left to be drawn through

it, Figs. 12, 13 (*cf.* the "Iris" of the East Pediment
of the Parthenon, British Museum, Elgin Room, No. G).

A third method, known by the name of the "Peplos
of Athena," since the goddess generally affects this form
of chiton, is given in Figs. 20, 21, 22. A glance

Fig. 19.—Procne and Philomela. From a Vase Painting.

at the scheme, Fig. 20, will make the arrangement
clear, and show that the girdle is put on over a
larger "apotygma" (or "folded-over piece") than in
scheme Fig. 8, and that no hanging bag, or κόλπος,
is drawn over the girdle. Fig. 21 is from the "Varvakeion" statuette, in the Central Museum at Athens,
which may be a far-away echo of the celebrated gold and

ivory statue set up by Pheidias in the Parthenon about
the middle of the fifth century B.C.   (A cast of the
Varvakeion statuette will be found in the corner of the
Elgin Room, British Museum, No. 300).   In Figs. 21,
22, over the peplos the goddess wears her "aegis," with
the head of Medusa in the centre of the chest.

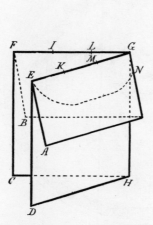

Fig. 20.—Scheme of the "Peplos   Fig. 21.—From the Varvakeion
        of Athena."   Statuette. Athens.

The Dorian chiton was made of fine wool, and was of a
kind more or less common to all Indo-Germanic tribes.
A modern parallel also still exists in the dress worn
by some Egyptian women (Fig. 23).   Very often a
sleeve is formed, in the Greek edition of the garment,
by placing buttons or pins at intervals from I K, L M,
downwards to the elbow (cf. the woman with the goat,

Fig. 24; or the woman with the child, Fig. 19; or the
so-called figure of " Alcestis," British Museum, Ephesus
Room, H 1). More elaborate girdlings formed by the
addition of extra cords crossed on the breast, and attached
to the ordinary girdle, are often found. (Fig. 25.)

On monuments it is not always easy sharply to dis-

Fig. 22.—Statuette of Athena.
Athens.

Fig. 23.—Dress of modern
Egyptian Woman.

tinguish the closed Dorian chiton from the variety that
must now be discussed, viz., the *Ionian chiton.* The chief
distinctive feature of the Dorian chiton consists in the
pins seen on the shoulders. From this peculiarity it
received the name περονατρίς (*cf.* Theocritus, xv., 21).

The Ionian chiton was entirely a sewn garment, with *no
pins.* It was made of linen, and came to Greece, more

especially to Athens, in the first half of the sixth century, from the Ionians of Asia Minor, who borrowed it from the peoples of Asia proper.

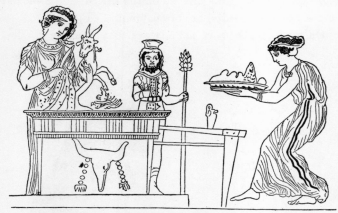

Fig. 24.—Illustration of Sleeve of Chiton, made by placing pins at intervals. From a Vase Painting.

A plan of it is given in Fig. 26. It will be seen that the piece of material, as a whole, is less than that required for the several varieties of the Dorian chiton, being at least a foot less in height. This garment may consist either of two pieces (one in front and one at back), or of one piece double the size and folded. Instead of the one side being closed by pins as in Fig. 14, these two pieces are joined, and both sides are closed by sewing at G C, H D,

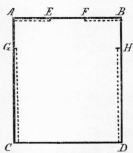

Fig. 26.—Scheme of the Ionian Chiton.

and also at the shoulders A E, F B, as indicated by the dotted lines. The distance from A to B being half the full span of the wearer with the arms stretched out, a long hanging sleeve is thus obtained (Fig. 27). The girdle is put on, as in the Dorian variety, and the extra length is drawn up through it so as to hang over and form a "kolpos." For an example of a girl arranging

Fig. 27.—Women wearing the Ionian Chiton. From a Vase Painting.

her own girdle, the reader may be referred to the vase from the Branteghem Collection lately acquired by the British Museum. (Third Vase Room, Turret Case C).

Good instances of this Ionian chiton may be studied in the British Museum Archaic Room, Cast No. 156, or on the figures of the so-called " Harpy Tomb," No. 94, in the same room. This dress seems to have been generally made of linen. The material, judging from the instances depicted on monuments, is of a finely crinkled kind, apparently elastic in nature, similar to a stuff still to be found among the home productions of modern Greece. It is finished off with a selvage, not a hem. This elastic material

Fig. 28.—Relief of the Charites (Graces). Vatican.

would close round the neck of a wearer of the Ionian chiton after the head had been inserted, as in the case of our modern vests and jerseys. A band of decoration is occasionally seen round the neck, as in Fig. 27.

The two great varieties of chiton, the Dorian and the Ionian, may be clearly seen side by side in Fig. 28, from the " Chiaramonti " collection in the Vatican, Rome, of which a cast will be found in the South Kensington collection (Perry's Catalogue, No. 54).

In this group of " Graces " the figure to the extreme left wears the ordinary closed Dorian chiton with " kolpos " and " apotygma," as given in Fig. 14. That in the centre has the same chiton, apparently open down the left side, and arranged as in Fig. 16, while the one to the right wears the Ionian chiton of Figs. 26, 27, made of the crinkled fine linen material just described.

In the two figures of this relief that wear the Dorian dress, I am bound to say I cannot see the pins as in Fig. 15, but the work of the relief is coarse and the style heavy, and it may only be an " archaistic " copy of an archaic original. The artist in such a case might not be very careful to represent exactly what he was copying, but there is small doubt of the fact of these two being instances of the Dorian chiton.

With regard to these two kinds of dress (the "Dorian " and the " Ionian ") Herodotus makes a definite statement in his history.[35] The land of the Epidaurians, he says, yielded no fruit, so the oracle at Delphi was consulted as to a remedy, and the Epidaurians were bidden to set up images of Damia and Auxesia (goddesses of increase). The material of which these statues were to be made was to be cultivated olive wood. The Epidaurians therefore besought the Athenians to allow them to take some from their olive-trees as they had a large supply. The petition was granted on condition of their sending, in return, yearly offerings to Athena Polias and Erechtheus in Athens. These terms were agreed upon, the wood was

[35] Herod., v., 82; cf. Pausanias, ii., xxx., 5.

cut, the statues carved, the gods appeased, and the earth of the Epidaurians yielded her fruit in due season.

But it came to pass that the Aeginetans subdued the Epidaurians by sea, and carried off the statues to their own land. Thereupon no more tribute was paid to Athens by the Epidaurians, and the Athenians, complaining of its cessation, were referred to the Aeginetans, who possessed the images. In consequence, the Athenians sent a company of men to Aegina to demand the statues. Their request was refused. Then force was tried, and the Athenians attempted to drag the images from their pedestals. But dreadful consequences ensued. It thundered, and the earth shook, the statues are said to have fallen upon their knees, and madness to have overtaken the men, so that they slew one another, and only one returned alive to Athens. When he got there and told his tale, the widows of the dead men were very indignant at his safety. They came round him demanding their lost husbands, and finally, in their rage, stabbed him with the pins, or clasps (περόνῃσι), of their garments till he died. The Athenians, in horror at the women's deed, as the most terrible punishment they could devise, changed the fashion of women's dress from the " Dorian " to the " Ionian," so that they might have no further need of clasps or pins, while the Greeks of Argos and Aegina made their fastenings larger than before.

As to this statement of the historian's there is little doubt that somewhere about 570 B.C., war was raging between the two always hostile peoples of Aegina and Athens, and that somewhere about the same time a change took place in the dress of Athenian women, and the fame of the two things was connected. From monumental evidence it would appear that one of the early forms of

women's dress is of a "sewn" kind, while dress on monuments that must be dated after the Persian Wars is of the
"Dorian" variety, as may be seen in the instances quoted
above, Figs. 10, 12, 13. The "Dorian," as Herodotus
points out (v., 88), was in all probability the old universal
dress of all Hellenic women. Afterwards in Athens, about
the first half of the sixth century, the so-called "Ionian"
kind came into fashion, and was in vogue, contemporaneously with the Dorian, till about the time of the
Persian Wars, 490—479 B.C. Then, in the wave of
renewed Hellenism which spread over Greece in the
national reaction against everything Eastern, the old
Hellenic fashion revived, bearing the name "Dorian"
(ἡ αὐτὴ ἦν τὴν νῦν Δωρίδα καλέομεν. Hdt. v. 88), because
it was among such conservative people as the Spartans
that it had been preserved.

But, strong as the reaction was, the "Ionian" dress
was not absolutely ousted from its place, since Oriental
influence was still too powerful for its radical rejec-
tion.

The original pin used for the fastening of garments
among early races appears to have been one made from
the small bone of the leg of an animal, whence the name
"fibula," or περόνη. This is next reproduced in metal,
furnished with a round head, and decorated with balls of
bronze, a characteristic Greek type of which may be seen
on the shoulder of the woman to the left in Fig. 5. In
some instances the point of such a pin has been bent back,
evidently to prevent its falling out of the garment when
once stuck in. It is a tempting hypothesis that from this
bending back of the point arose that developed form of
"fibula" of which the modern "safety-pin" is the direct

and almost unmodified descendant. Such safety-pins in bronze have lately been discovered at Mycenae during the works carried on by the Greek Archæological Society in 1888 and following years.[36] Fibulae occur among the oldest bronzes of Olympia, as will be seen in the works of Drs. Furtwängler and Curtius, published by the German Archæological Institute, and included in the list of books in my Introduction. They are also found in the early graves of Thebes, Athens, Austria, Sicily, and other places. Golden fibulae (περόναι) are mentioned in Homer (as in *Il.* v. 425, &c.), but it is difficult to determine whether the Homeric form is that of the straight pin or the " safety-pin."

Most representations on vases seem to depict in long or short variety the characteristic Greek type of pin found in tombs (*cf.* Fig. 5). The " safety-pin " type, for some reason, seems almost or altogether absent from Greek tombs of the sixth and fifth century B.C.

Wounds would be more deadly and more easily inflicted by such pins as those of Fig. 5 than by the point of a " safety-pin." The Greek tragedians mention dresses worn by women both with and without pins. Polyxena, in the *Hecuba* of Euripides, takes hold of her dress near the shoulder and tears it open to the waist, implying a sewn garment that could not be simply unpinned at the shoulder ; but in the same play Polymnestor is blinded by means of the pins or brooches (πόρπη = περόνη) that the women take from their garments for the purpose. In

[36] *Cf.* Schuchhardt, *op. cit.* pp. 296, 313 ; Daremberg and Saglio's " Dictionnaire," art. " Fibula," p. 2004, Fig. 2977 ; and Montelius " Archiv für Anthropologie," Brunswick, 1892, p. 31, Fig. 35.

the *Persae* of Aeschylus (*circa* 472 B.C.) Hellas wears the "Dorian" as the real Greek dress.

Some typical instances of the developed "safety-pin" form of fibula are given full-size in Fig. 29, *a, b, c, d,* from my husband's collection.

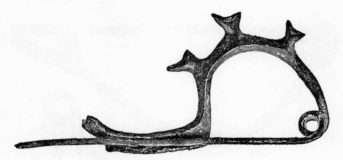

Fig. 29 (*a*).

Fig. 29 (*b*).

Existing specimens of pins and fibulae may be studied in any good collection, such as that in the Bronze Room of the British Museum, or in the Ashmolean Museum, Oxford. Those of very large size in these col-

lections may not have been worn, but were perhaps used
for " ex-votos," or offerings in temples,[37] or for fastening
curtains or other decorative hangings, or, as they are
found in graves, they may have been made for the decoration of the dead.   A fibula from Halstatt belonging to my
husband was evidently made for funeral purposes, as it

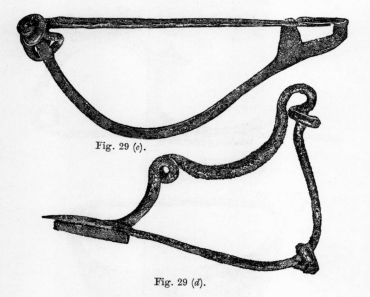

Fig. 29 (c).

Fig. 29 (d).

still contains some of the clay used as a core in its manufacture, and the edge of its decoration still feels sharp
and rough to the finger, in evidence that it was not worn
previously to its interment.

In later times, when the conquests of Alexander had let
loose a new flood of Orientalism on Greece, the "Ionian"
style with many rich varieties of Eastern decoration

[37] Hdt., v. 88.

seems to have been largely worn. (*Cf.* Fig. 30.) This figure, however, represents Medea, who can perhaps be hardly counted among the pure Greeks. Other instances of rich dress may be found in the British Museum

Fig. 30.—Medea. From a Vase Painting.

Fig. 31.—Amazon. Berlin Museum.

(Fourth Vase Room. Case 18. Vase signed by Python (no number), and case 54, F 326, and F 117 pedestal case.)

The *short chiton* of the women is also found on monu-

D

ments, together with the long. It follows the longer
style in its varieties of sewing, pinning, and arranging,
but it is not so full, and only reaches to the knee. It is
worn by women and girls engaged in active exercise or
when speed is desired. Iris the messenger, Artemis the
huntress, girls in running contests and warring Amazons,
all wear it. Instances are numerous in the frieze from
the Mausoleum, Halicarnassos, in the British Museum, of
which casts exist at South Kensington (Perry's Catalogue,
No. 137). Others are given in Figs. 25, 31, 32.

Sometimes (*cf.* Fig. 32) it is fastened on one shoulder
only, and the figure is supported by a broad belt. This
statue may represent one of the girls who used, according
to Pausanias (v. 16, 2), to take part in a race at the
Festival of Hera at Olympia, wearing a garment that
hardly reached to the knee and left the right shoulder and
part of the breast uncovered. The race was run in the
stadium, but only over one-sixth of the course. In
Fig. 31, a second belt is put on over the top of the
" kolpos," or bag of material drawn up through the girdle
beneath it.

Fig. xxv. Detail from black-figured hydria (ca. 560 B.C.)
British Museum. Odysseus and his men blinding the
Cyclops.

III.

DRESS OF THE FEMALE FIGURES IN THE ACROPOLIS MUSEUM, ATHENS.

At this point, before proceeding to a discussion of the dress of the men of Greece in historic times and the outer garments (*epiblemata*) of both men and women, it will be well, I think, to notice the garments on that remarkable series of statues of archaic female figures, found in the course of the excavations conducted on the Acropolis, under the direction of M. Cavvadias in the years 1882-8, of which a description is given in M. Collignon's *History of Greek Sculpture*,[38] and in Professor Gardner's book.[39]

These statues, which were discovered between the Erechtheum and the north boundary wall of the Acropolis, have, owing to the variety of surfaces represented in their garments and their brilliant colouring, attracted much attention and have given rise to opposite opinions. Their brilliant polychromatic decoration is very remarkable, hair, eyes, and borders of garments sharing in the

[38] *Histoire de la Sculpture Grecque*, M. Collignon, p. 340, &c.
[39] *New Chapters in Greek History*, Percy Gardner, p. 247, &c. (*Cf.* Cavvadias' *Les Musées d'Athènes*, and the "ἐφημερὶς ἀρχαιολογική," 1883—88).

colours which do not always follow natural laws ; for
instance, the eyes of the figures are sometimes coloured
red, a tint that seems, to our notions, most abnormal and
undesirable.

I have on an earlier page spoken of the great difficulty
of giving precise dates in Greek art. In the case of these
figures this difficulty is, to a great extent, removed.
After the Acropolis was sacked by the Persians in 480 B.C.,
and, spoiled and ruined, had once more come into the
hands of its rightful owners, the victorious Greeks buried
the fragments of statues and other objects that had decorated their citadel before its spoliation.

This was done partly in reverence to the gods, since
anything once dedicated to a deity was always sacred and
could not be put to profane usage ; partly to hide the
traces of the Oriental invaders' brief triumph ; and partly
from utilitarian motives to increase the level space on the
summit of the Acropolis, since, in the full spring of
renewed patriotism, the Athenians desired to make " all
things new," and required other and enlarged temples
filled with fresh statues. Probably many of the objects
found in these excavations had only just been made at the
time of their destruction. Be this as it may, the last of
the series, which ranges over a considerable period of time,
cannot be later than 480 B.C. One of the series, Fig. 33,
is held to belong to a base inscribed with the name of
the sculptor Antenor.[39a] With regard to this artist we
know that he made the statues of Harmodius and Aristo-
geiton, who slew the tyrant Hipparchus, 514 B.C. Those
statues must have been set up soon after the murder, and

[39a] Cf. Collignon's *Histoire*, p. 365 and ἐφημ : ἀρχ : 1886 ;
No. 6, Pl. IV., p. 81 ; and C. I. A. iv. 373.

probably the Acropolis figure to which the Antenor base is ascribed is of the same period. By this means we get two points of date for the Acropolis series, viz., B.C. 480 back to *circa* B.C. 514—510. Another of the series may, on the evidence of style, even go back to 600 B.C. Fourteen of these figures came to light at once in February, 1886, having been buried together in a single pit, and others were found later. The series has given rise to much discussion as to whether the figures represent portraits of the priestesses of the goddess, of the actual goddess, or of the votaries who dedicated the images. Whomsoever they are intended to represent, they doubtless portray for us the costume of Athenian ladies of good position in the years preceding the great Persian invasion of 480 B.C. Some of the more typical varieties of dress found on them are given in Figs. 34, 35, 36. It cannot, however, be denied that the sculptor has allowed himself considerable latitude in the treatment of the garments. In consequence of this latitude two schools of disputants on their dress have arisen, the one typified by M. Lechat,[40] the other by Dr. Müller.[41] It is evident to the most casual observer that the drapery is not always true to actual fact, the curves going across the body when in repose in a way that could only be produced by rapid motion.[42] Again, it is not unusual to find a garment that shows some special and well-defined pattern or border covering one part of the body, while where we should expect to find the same garment continued, another pattern or

[40] *Bulletin de Corr. Hell.*, 1890.

[41] *Quaestiones Vestiariae.* W. Müller.

[42] See notes on these figures, by Ernest Gardner, in the *Journal of Hellenic Studies*, viii. 1, p. 170.

border suddenly comes out without apparent reason. There can be little doubt that the upper and lower portions of such a dress (*endyma*) do really belong to one and the same garment—the Ionian chiton—with sleeves close fitting and often elaborately bordered, while over this is thrown the ordinary himation (*epiblema*). But some archæologists (like M. Lechat, already mentioned) have endeavoured to make out a separate garment for every piece represented by a different pattern or border till, by this means, each figure seems to be clothed in three or four separate garments, of a kind otherwise unknown, for which distinctive titles have to be invented. To such critics a difference of *pattern* always implies a difference of *material.* Thus for Fig. 34, the existence of an under-chiton and a "chitoniscus," or knitted vest put over the chiton under the himation is assumed.

For my own part, I must confess that, in spite of its apparent absurdity, the possibility of such a multiplication of garments as that indicated by M. Lechat, and adopted by M. Collignon, did remain in my mind, until in April, 1892, I had the good fortune, in the course of a cruise among the Greek islands, to visit the rough wooden shed that does duty for a museum in the little island of Mykonos, where are housed some fragments of the objects found on neighbouring sites. There, with some difficulty, owing to the intense interest taken in our visit by every man, woman, and child of the place, I came across a piece of sculpture that, to my mind, solved the question. I found a headless female figure, apparently belonging to the same period of art, and dressed in the same manner as the Acropolis statues, *i.e.* in the Ionian chiton, with a himation over it. On

the left breast of the figure, for a space of about six
inches square, without the slightest semblance of a join
in the material of the chiton, the sculptor had suddenly
changed the pattern of the garment·stuff from one of
three deeply-crinkled lines, with interspaces of plain
material, to a patch of close and continuous wavy lines
with no interspaces. Unfortunately, so far as I know,
this figure is not published, and I cannot give an illustration of it. But after my visit to Mykonos, I found,
in the Acropolis Museum at Athens, a similar instance
on a female statue (No. 598 in the official catalogue,
edit. 1891), and the same thing may be noticed in Fig.
35, where the lines of the pattern coalesce on the right
side in a way impossible in fact. Since then I have had it
brought to my notice, in an excellent article by Dr.
Hauser,[43] that the same is the case in the dress of the so-
called "Woman getting into a Chariot" (cast in British
Museum, Archaic Room, No. 155), where the sleeve only
of an under-garment that falls in heavy folds to the feet
is shown with a crinkled surface, the remainder being
smooth. This figure (be it a woman or a male charioteer)
seems to me, as Dr. Hauser suggests, to wear a long,
linen, sleeved, "Ionian" chiton, with a shawl-like wrap
over it. These differences of creased or crinkled surface,
therefore, occurring irregularly, do not represent a difference of material, and consequently a separate garment, but are attempts to show the various ways in which
the same garment may appear, owing to the folds which
it assumes and the shape of the body it covers; falling
in close, fine folds over the chest and shoulders, and in

[43] *Jahrbuch des Kais. Deutsch. Arch. Inst.* vii. 1, 1892,
p. 55.

larger, freer style over the legs (Fig. 37). Other
instances, both in sculpture and vase-painting, might be
cited.

By this view the "chitoniscus" of Lechat and Boehlau,[44] or the "wollene Wams" of the catalogue of
vases in the Berlin collection, by Dr. Furtwängler, disappears as a separate garment, and becomes merely the
upper portion of the Ionian chiton, arranged over the
girdle in a "kolpos," in the manner described in my
previous chapter, Figs. 26, 27. There is little doubt
that the "chitoniscus," mentioned by classical writers,[44a]
is the short form of chiton given above (Figs. 25, 31, 32).

In the case of artists who could so indiscriminately use
their colours as to paint the eyes of a woman red, as the
sculptors of the Acropolis figures did, it seems an affectation to imagine that the lines and patterns on the garments, graved by their tools and coloured by their brush,
must necessarily be exactly true to reality. It is, therefore, unwise to argue from their productions a subservience
to the exact representation of actual material, only to be
equalled in the work of the draughtsman of the modern
fashion-plate. In such early art as that of the period to
which these figures belong the artist was free and untrammelled, and could change at will from one pattern to
another in the same garment, without thereby giving
good grounds for inferring that the material was really
different. The fact that the garments themselves of this
series vary in a parallel manner cannot be taken to count

[44] Cf. Boehlau's *Quaestiones de re vestiaria Graecorum*, fig.
14, p. 38, &c.

[44a] *E.g.* by Aristoph. *Birds*, 946, 955; Demosth., 583, 21,
403, &c.

for much as evidence, since, whomsoever they may represent, they were dedicated to the divinity, and the intense
conservatism of the Greeks in matters of religion is well
known.

That these statues vary from each other as much as
they do is an important advance on statues of the
class that precedes them—a class marked by an almost
unvarying similarity of treatment down to the smallest
details.

One figure of the series, Fig. 38, by exception, seems
to wear the Dorian chiton, very stiffly depicted. The
girdle is noticeable for curious hanging bands depending
from it to relieve the severity of the drapery.

The outer garment of these female figures is the ordinary himation that I shall shortly describe. In these
instances it is often passed under the left arm and, crossing the chest, secured on the right shoulder (Figs. 35,
36). Sometimes it is laid over both shoulders like a cloak
(Fig. 34). In either case the himation seems of a shape
more oblong than the square it usually assumes. The
exact regularity of the zigzag folds is not necessarily
true to life, as these folds occur everywhere in Greek art
of a certain period, and are the results of a rigid archaism
and conventionality. The curious way in which the arm
comes from out of the cloak (Fig. 34), without causing
any such hanging folds as would be expected, may either
be another instance of the artist's limitations, or the
garment may have been scalloped in some manner or
holes cut in it to allow the arms to pass through.

Across the breast in Figs. 35, 36, some of the length
of the himation seems drawn up through the band caused
by its being fastened tightly on the shoulder, and a frill-

like effect is thus gained. The key to this arrangement
is found in the right-hand figure of the Chiaramonti
relief (Fig. 28), where its scheme can be very plainly
made out.

The chitons worn by the Acropolis figures (*cf.* Fig.
34) are girdled in the same manner as that suggested for
putting on the Ionian chiton, but after the " kolpos "
or bag has been drawn up, the folds of the " petticoat "
part are neatly arranged in pleats. Sometimes in this
series, as on the right shoulder of Fig. 35 no very rigid
distinction is made between the lines of the chiton and
the himation.

Fig. xxvi. Kore by Antenor. Athens, Acropolis Museum. Re-
storative drawing.

IV.

UNDER-GARMENTS OF THE MEN.

HERODOTUS, in his narrative mentioned above, is, as we have seen, only concerned with the dress of Hellenic women.[45] Thucydides, in the archæological preface to his history,[46] deals with the dress of the men.

His words are as follows :—[47] " The fashion of wearing arms among these continental tribes is a relic of their old predatory habits. For in ancient times all Hellenes carried weapons because their homes were undefended and intercourse was unsafe. . . . They went armed in their everyday life. And the continuance of the custom in certain parts of the country proves that it once prevailed everywhere. The Athenians were the first who laid aside arms and adopted a more easy and luxurious way of life. Quite recently the old-fashioned refinement of dress still lingered among the elder men of their richer class, who wore under-garments of linen and bound back their hair in a knot with golden clasps in the form of grasshoppers (Gr. τεττίγων). The same customs long survived among the elders of Ionia, having been derived from their Athenian ancestors.

[45] Hdt., v., 82.   [46] Thuc., i., 6.
[47] Professor Jowett's translation.

" On the other hand the simple dress which is now common was first worn at Sparta, and there, more than anywhere else, the life of the rich was assimilated to that of the people."

This review of the dress of Greek men by Thucydides falls into three periods:—

(1.) The oldest period, when armour was universally worn in ordinary life, a period to which the references in Homer may belong with more or less accuracy—a fashion preserved in Thucydides' day (B.C. *circ.* 471— 404) only in the country parts of Greece, as Epirus, Acarnania, and the like.

(2.) The succeeding period when, as he puts it, "men adopted a more easy and luxurious way of life," probably denoting by these words that influx of Oriental customs from Ionia typified by the linen chiton of the women (the " Ionian chiton " of Chapter II.) worn also by men, and the wearing of the long hair bound with gold.

(3.) The fashion of the date of the outbreak of the Peloponnesian War in 431 B.C., " the present fashion " (ὁ νῦν τρόπος) of Thucydides' day, *i.e.* the simple so-called " Dorian " chiton, made of woollen material, a revival from older days, due to the Hellenic reaction against Orientalism after the victory over the Persians, B.C. 480—79.

Wool probably then became the prevailing fashion, partly as " un-Oriental," and partly as being considered more healthy at a period when the " sound mind in sound body " was the aim of the Athenian state on behalf of her citizens. The hair at this period, too, was cut short, giving more freedom and ease.

The short woollen chiton of the third period was a

moderately wide garment on the same lines as the Dorian chiton of the women given in Fig. 8, with the part below the girdle sewn together, the upper part left open and fastened on the shoulders with fibulae or buttons. The girdling was done in the same way as for the women, but there seems to have been no " folded-over " piece or "apotygma," such as was general in their case.

But, contemporaneously with this practical and useful garment of everyday life, the longer and more dignified linen chiton of the Period II. of Thucydides was retained as a dress for religious and festival occasions in which men took part. .

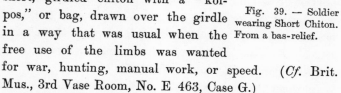

Period III. of Thucydides, therefore, carries on many of the characteristics of Period II., but puts them on a basis of solemnity, retaining them in the service of religion—always the most conservative of mistresses.

In Fig. 39 the soldier wears the short, girdled chiton with a "kol-pos," or bag, drawn over the girdle in a way that was usual when the free use of the limbs was wanted

Fig. 39. — Soldier wearing Short Chiton. From a bas-relief.

for war, hunting, manual work, or speed.   (*Cf.* Brit. Mus., 3rd Vase Room, No. E 463, Case G.)

In the text of Hartwig's *Meisterschalen*, mentioned in the list of books in my Introduction, there occurs, at p. 219, Fig. 30*b*, an instance from a painting on a vase representing a youth putting on a short chiton. This dress is very curiously drawn as if the wearer was about to put it on *after* it has been drawn in at the waist by a girdle. The lines of the folds of the chiton, too, above the waist are differently drawn to those below; but I hope I have said enough to prove that this need not necessarily denote two sorts of material. With regard to the chiton having the appearance of being already drawn in at the waist before being put on, Dr. Hartwig makes the ingenious suggestion that it is probably due to the fact that the artist was accustomed to see the chiton so drawn in when in wear, and therefore so depicted it when he wished to represent it in process of being put on.

Artisans and fisher-folk fastened the short chiton on one shoulder only, the left, when the name ἐξωμίς (exomis) was given to it. Charon, the ferryman, so wears it in Fig. 40.[47a] (Cf. Brit. Mus. 3rd Vase Room, No. D 24, Case F.)

The long chiton remained at the same period (c. 431 B.C.) as the dress of men of middle life and distinguished rank. It was also worn by younger men when engaged in certain functions, as, for instance, when acting as priests, flute-players, or charioteers. For a figure of a charioteer so clothed, of a period slightly later than this, the reader is referred to the slab, perhaps the most beautiful of the whole series, from the Mausoleum, British Museum, Mausoleum Room (cast at South Kensington, Perry's Catalogue, No. 137).

In the chitons on vases of the late Black-figured and Red-figured periods the same fine fan-like folds are discernible that can be noticed in the Acropolis figures (Figs. 34, 35, 36). Endless instances will reward the student who looks, even casually, through the 2nd and 3rd Vase Rooms of the British Museum. They are pro-

---

[47a] ἑτερομάσχαλος χιτὼν δουλικὸς, ἥν ἐξωμίδα λέγουσι, Photius, s.v.

bably due to the artist's desire to show his skill, and to
archaic conventionality. But some German critics have
conjectured that these folds were actually so worn and

Fig. 40.—Charon, wearing the "exomis."

produced by some artificial process akin to our plan of
starching, goffering, or ironing. The evidence for such a
practice in the case of the Greeks does not, I believe,
exist, though similar customs were well known in Egypt.

OUTER GARMENTS OF BOTH MEN AND WOMEN
OF GREECE IN HISTORIC TIMES.

UNDER this head come all kinds of garments put on in shawl or wrap fashion both by men and women, to which the general term "epiblemata" (ἐπιβλήματα) was applied.

The chief of these garments is the *Himation* (ἱμάτιον), to which I have from time to time referred in the foregoing pages. The "chlaina" (χλαῖνα), of Homeric times must have been merely a variety of the himation.

Both men and women seem to have worn a himation of the same shape—a large square, sometimes rather oblong than square, varying in size according to the taste of the wearer and the state of the weather. Both sexes followed in the main the rules of arrangement given below, but the women did not adhere so rigidly as the men to these rules, and were addicted to coquettish variations in their draperies. Their himation must usually have been larger than that worn by the men, since it was often drawn over the head as a covering. Figs. 41 and 42, terra-cottas from Tanagra, Bœotia, illustrate this use. Fig. 43, a slab now in the Central Museum at Athens, shows another pretty way of arranging the folds. In deep grief the mantle was used to completely muffle the figure of the wearer. Demeter, in the Homeric hymn, when going to Metaneira's house as an old nurse, is " wrapped and covered from head to foot so that her dark

Fig. 41.—Terra·cotta figurine from Tanagra.

Fig. 42.—Terra-cotta figurine from Tanagra.

robe clung to her as she walked." The general rule for putting on the himation in classical times seems to have been as follows :—One corner of the square, or oblong, was folded or gathered up and grasped by the hand and pulled

E

over the left shoulder from the back, then tucked in
securely and held firmly between the body and the left
upper arm pressed against the ribs. Then, with the
right hand, the mantle was pulled out across the wearer's
back by its right-hand top corner, opposite the corner
already secured, till the lower edge of the garment
hung about half way across the calf of the leg. Then
the wrap was brought round over the right side of
the body (ἐπιδέξια)[48] to the front, when two ways of
disposing of this right-hand corner were possible, viz. :
(A) If the right hand and arm were wanted to be free,
the himation was brought *under* the right shoulder, drawn
across the chest, and the end thrown over the left
shoulder. (B) In the way considered the more suitable
for honourable citizens, the mantle was brought *over* the
right arm and shoulder (the arm being bent at the elbow)
so that only the right hand appeared in a sling-like fold
in the front, and then the end was thrown over the left
shoulder. Fig. 44, from the well-known figure of the
Sophocles of the Lateran, illustrates this second method.

The youth in Fig. 45 has begun to put his himation on
in the first method, but, standing at ease, the superfluous
end has slipped from his left shoulder to his arm. To us
who find it necessary to use pins if we try to drape a
himation for a wearer who has to move rapidly on the
stage or elsewhere, it is matter for marvel *how* the ancient
Greeks kept theirs in position. The himation was the
dress of the dignified citizen, and he, though an excitable
Southern in disposition, had to learn to control his feelings
in a suitable fashion. Aristotle, in his picture of the
great and high-souled gentleman, takes it for granted

[48] Plato, *Thaeet.*, 175 E., ἐπιδέξια ἀναβάλλεσθαι ἐλευθέρως.

Fig. xxvii. Statuette of snake godess. Crete, Museum of Herakleion. Found at excavations of Palace of Minos at Knossos. Jacket bares breasts, belt, apron effect of dress, tiered skirt.

PLATE LL

Fig. xxviii. Archaic statue of goddess (ca. 380 B.C.) Berlin
National Museum. Goddess wears diadem, hairnet, himation as a shawl and long Ionian chiton.

Fig. 9.— From the Great Altar, Pergamos.

Fig. 10.—Figure of a Hesperid.   Olympia.

Fig. 25.—Amazon, with crossed bands from the girdle.   Athens.

Fig. 17.—Bronze figure from Herculaneum.

Naples Museum.

Fig. 32.—The " Running Girl."

Vatican.

Fig. 43.—Slab. Central Museum, Athens.

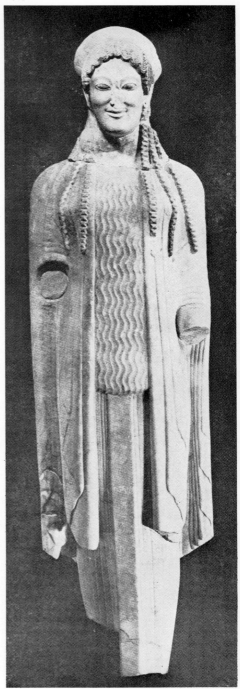

g. 33.—Figure ascribed to a base with the
name of the artist Antenor.   Athens.

Fig. 34.— Female figure discovered
on the Acropolis.   Athens.

Fig. 35.—Female figure discovered on the Acropolis.   Athens.

Fig. 36.—Female figure discovered on the Acropolis.
Athens.

Fig. 38.—Female figure found on the
Acropolis. Athens.

Fig. 52.—Stele of Hegeso. Athens.

PLATE VV

Fig. 70.—Female figure found on the Acropolis.   Athens.

xxix.

xxx.

xxxi.

xxxii.

xxxiii.

Fig. xxix. Head from terra cotta statuette of Demeter (4th c. B.C.) Chicago Natural History Museum. Goddess wears a diadem.

Fig. xxx. Head from terra cotta statuette of woman (ca. 3rd c. B.C.) Chicago Natural History Museum. Possibly from Alexandria. See hairdress and round earrings.

Fig. xxxi. Fragment from terra cotta statuette of boy (late 3rd c. B.C.) Chicago Natural History Museum. Boy wears hat and heavy sleeveless cloak.

Fig. xxxii. Head from statuette of boy (late 3rd c. B.C,) Chicago Natural History Museum. Boy has "bowl" hair-cut and wears hat.

Fig. xxxiii. Head from statuette of Isis. Chicago Natural History Museum. Goddess wears hair parted in center and dressed with a polos, a diadem, veil and earrings.

PLATE XX

Fig. xxxiv. Terra cotta statuette of woman from Tanagra.
Berlin National Museum. Woman wears large flat hat,
cloak and chiton and carries a fan.

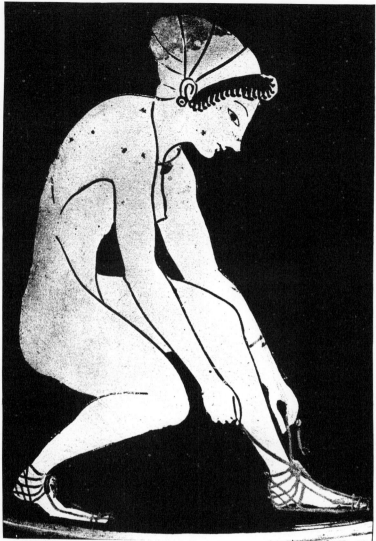

Fig. xxxv. Detail from red-figured amphora (ca. 530 B.C.)
Paris, Louvre Museum. Woman binding sandal.

Fig. xxxvi. Sandal. London, Guildhall
Museum. Found preserved in mud of
Thames. (ca. 1st c. A.D,?)

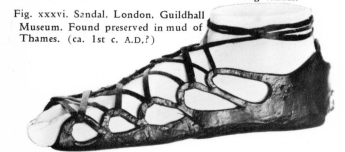

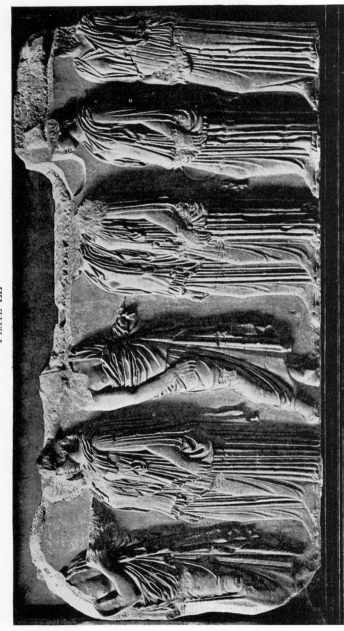

Fig. xxxvii. Procession of maidens from Parthenon frieze. Paris, Louvre Museum. Maidens are dressed in long Ionian chitons.

that it would not become him to walk "swinging his
arms about."[48]   But all the same it would be very clever
of anyone, however dignified, to keep a himation well in
position through a long day in the jury-courts or the
senate of Athens, without a sly pin inserted craftily some-

Fig. 45.—Penelope and Telemachos.   From a Vase Painting.

where to keep his drapery steady.   Little weights of clay
or lead fastened to the corners of garments were certainly
used.[49]   The himation, however, may have been thrown
on and off at will, or readjusted from time to time.   But
the arrangement of this garment was always considered

[48] Aris., *Nic. Eth.*, iv., 3—15.
[49] *Cf.* Figs. 21, 22, 45, 50 (Frontispiece).

a difficulty, requiring practice and assistance. A man's character and culture were judged from its folds. In the "Characters" of Theophrastus the boor's himation does not reach to his knee; the oligarch goes about with his gracefully adjusted. Alcibiades is said to have let his trail behind him.

The narrow doubled himation may be seen on archaic

Fig. 46.—From the
François Vase.

vases, as, for example, in the British Museum, 2nd Vase Room, No. B 197, Case K. Another instance from the François vase (Fig. 46) has been taken to be of Ionian origin, coming in with the longer Ionian chiton, which did not require so complete an outside wrap as the shorter Dorian chiton of the men. But still it is found on some of the oldest vases (from one of which our figure is taken), and women on the most archaic

Attic vases also wear it put on cloak-wise from the back. A curious survival of it to later classical days may be noticed in the dress of the maidens of the Parthenon frieze (British Museum, Elgin Room, No. 324, Slabs VII., VIII., Figs. 52—60), the figure of the Caryatid of the Erechtheum (same room, No. 407 given in Fig. 47) and in the "Eirene" of Munich, reproduced here in Fig. 48. They, it will be noticed, wear the Dorian chiton of Fig. 14 with apotygma, kolpos, and shoulder-fastening complete. But these shoulder-fastenings are made to do double duty and to support an extra piece of oblong drapery at the back—in fact the long, narrow himation of older days now fixed securely instead of coming cloak-wise over the shoulders as in the dress of the Acropolis statue, Fig. 34.

The *chlamys* (χλαμύς) was another wrap for men's use, originating in Thessaly as a rider's dress worn over armour. From the fifth century onwards it was universal in Greece.

Fig. 47. — Caryatid. British Museum.   Fig. 48.—Eirene, with infant Ploutos. Munich.

It was a short light mantle, made of wool, oblong in shape, with square or rounded corners, fastened with a clasp either in front or on the right shoulder. With the "Petasos" (or flat traveller's hat with flaps), it became the general dress for young men of "Ephebos" standing (*i.c.* "just at the threshold of manhood") in Athens,

serving in the cavalry. Endless instances of this dress can be discovered in the frieze of the Parthenon in the British Museum. An example from a vase painting is given in Fig. 49. (*Cf.* British Museum, 3rd Vase Room, Case A, No. E 3.)

Gods of "Ephebos age" in art, as Hermes and Apollo, and men both young and old wear the chlamys, if engaged in active pursuits. Boys below this age wear a wide himation (Fig. 50, Frontispiece), quite covering the person, since it was not correct for a boy of good rank to have his

Fig. 49.—Youth in Chlamys.

hands free—perhaps a wise precaution for other nations than the Greeks. Infants were closely swaddled in modern Italian fashion and wore conical caps (Fig. 51).

Fig. 51.—Greek Babies.　Terra-cottas from Bœotia.

In Sparta, from their twelfth year onwards, men wore

winter and summer as an only dress, the *Tribon* (τρίβων),
i.e. the small oblong shawl of the Doric tribes. This was
also worn in Athens as a special dress for active military
work. But in the city this old dress, except for such
occasions, was considered boorish and affected, and was
only worn by philosophers and persons of peculiar views.
It was not correct for a dignified citizen to go beyond his
own door in the chiton only
without an upper garment. It
was also considered improper to
wear chlamys or himation without the chiton. Yet instances of
such wearing of one garment
only are undoubtedly found in
art, and some of them are
figured in these pages, as, for
example, the Sophocles of Fig.
44.

These may only be instances of
artistic latitude and of the desire,
at the fine period in Greek art,
to show as much as possible of
the human form, for in real life
in Athens only poor people and
philosophers wore the upper
without the under garment in
public or *vice versâ*.[49a]

Fig. 51*a*.—"Diana of
Gabii." Fastening the
Diplax.

A pretty variety of outdoor wrap for women, very
much on the lines of the men's "chlamys," is the
"diplax" (δίπλαξ) of Fig. 51*a*, where, as its name implies,
the garment is "doubled" before being adjusted.

[49a] *Cf.* Dio. *Chr. Or.*, lxxxii., p. 628, M. Xen. Mem., 1, 6, 2.

The custom of doubling the himation that prevailed among men in early times has already been mentioned at page 52 (Fig. 46.).

Curious isolated instances of garments are often found represented in Greek art, especially in vase paintings. They are difficult to classify, and have rather to be considered individually. They occur in almost any collection. In the British Museum I would refer the student to a consideration of the curious jacket worn by the woman on the Vase E 120, Case 25 ; or to the chequered top garment that looks almost as if distended by artificial means worn by the flute-player on the Vase E 286, Turret Case H.

When trousers are found in Greek art they denote un-Greek peoples, as Scythians or Persians. Long sleeves to the wrist are, in the case of women, a mark of the slave. In the accompanying Fig. 52, from a tombstone relief in the Central Museum, Athens (cast in the British Museum, Phigaleia Room, No. 619), the maid, in a long-sleeved dress, is assisting her mistress to prepare her toilet for the last time. When men are represented as wearing long sleeves they are generally foreigners. The origin of such sleeves may be assigned to the fashion of the Asiatic Greeks. On the Tower of the Winds, Athens, the fierce outlandish god of the north-west wind (Skiron) and his fellow of the north (Boreas), wear long sleeves. An instance of a young man, however, who is presumably Athenian, but who may after all be merely a colonist possibly from the Euxine, in a long-sleeved chiton, will be found in the British Museum (Elgin Room, Parthenon Frieze, No. 325, Slab 42, Fig. 109).

VI.

GIRDLES, FABRICS, COVERINGS FOR THE HEAD AND FEET, ETC.

THE girdle was an important part of the women's dress in Homeric times. Those of Calypso and of Circe seem to have been decorated with gold.[50]

This custom of decoration of the girdle lasted on to classical times. The Acropolis figure, No. 38, has her girdle decorated with pendent ornaments, very probably of leather, with gold or silver studs, in the way that Greek peasants' belts are decorated at the present time. The figure given in cut No. 7, wears a girdle fringed below the waist. The height of the girdling of the chiton in Greek art varies at different times and is a fairly safe guide for assigning a date to monuments. In archaic times, when found with the stiff, narrow foldless garments of the Black-figured vases it is at the waist line. At the period of the finest art (*circa* B.C. 450), it is slightly lower, as may be noticed in the dress of the maidens of the Parthenon frieze. Gradually, after this time the girdle creeps up, till at the period of the frieze of

---

[50] *Od.*, v., 231; *Od.*, x., 544, &c.

the great altar of Pergamos, Fig. 53 (*circa* B.C. 200—168), it has almost reached the arm-pits.

With regard to material there is considerable difference at different times; and a certain amount of evidence as to the date of Greek monuments can be extracted from the stuff of which garments appear to be made. As I have already mentioned, in quite early art and up to the time of the Persian invasions, 480 B.C., chitons are frequently made of a soft crinkled material, very like crape, edged with a woven selvage which drapes beautifully. But this material goes out of use about the time of Pheidias. It was no doubt very like the crape-like material still woven in the Greek islands, and procurable in Athens, very elastic and fine. I have slept in a peasant's cottage in Arcadia in fine creamy crape-like sheets, each sheet finished off with selvages, and the crape lines occasionally crossed with single threads of red or even of gold. This was in a village where old forms were very likely to have come down from remote times. There the peasant proprietor existed in an ideal fashion, and nearly everything in his house was made by the family itself or in the village, an excellent example of Aristotle's αὐτάρκεια, or "self-containedness."

Apart from the use of wool and linen, a sort of cotton (Byssus) was used for head-dresses and smaller pieces of the women's dress. It grew in Elis, was rather yellow in colour, and so expensive that its use for large garments must have been out of the question. Some of the earliest gold staters of Tarentum have as their obverse a beautiful head of Demeter or Persephone-Gaia wearing a stephane from which hangs a diaphanous veil. This veil is doubtless the Ταράντιον or Ταραντινίδιον, woven from the "byssus" of the " Pinna " shell, a form of textile industry that still survives among the inhabitants of modern Taranto.[51]

After the time of Pheidias, the woven selvage of garments seems to have been cut off, and the edges finished with the ordinary hem. This may be noticed on the drapery hanging by the Hermes of Praxiteles at Olympia. (Cast in the British Museum, Ephesus Room, No. K 2, also in the South Kensington Cast Collection, Perry's Catalogue, No. 114.) This hem does away with a great deal of the grace of the falling folds of the Parthenon draperies (as No. 324, Slabs VII., VIII., Figs 50—60) making the edge much clumsier and stiffer.

Finest of all materials must have been the muslins of Amorgos which are mentioned in Attic Comedy, and were no doubt extraordinarily dear.[52] These, together with the garments from Cos, remarkable for their transparency, and frequently mentioned by authors, specially by the Latin poets of the Augustan age,[53] were worn, in all probability, chiefly by the class of the " hetairae," though respectable married ladies may have used them in the extreme heat, in the strict privacy of the house. On vases of the severe and fine Red-figured period it is very usual to find the forms of the body showing through the garments. This may reflect a current fashion of transparent garments, or it may be due to an artistic custom of drawing the nude figure on the clay, before clothing it with appropriate draperies.

[51] *Cf.* Pliny., N.H., xix., 20, J. E. Forster *de Bysso Antiquorum*, London, 1776 ; and *The Horsemen of Tarentum*, by Arthur J. Evans in the *Numismatic Chronicle*, 3rd series, vol. ix., 1889, p. 66.

[52] Aristoph., *Lysist.*, 736.

[53] Hor., *Carm.*, iv., 13, 13 ; Ov., *Ars Am.*, ii., 298.

Silk has been supposed by some critics to have been
the material of which the "Coae vestes" were composed.
It certainly seems to have been spun and woven at Cos
at an early period,[54] but it was rare and dear in Alexandrian times, and not improbably imported from the
East.   Mr. Rennell Rodd notes the present silk industry
of modern Greece[55] at Achmetaga, a village in Euboea,
"an industry of historic antiquity in Greece which might
be much developed in a country where the mulberry
tree flourishes as it does here."   Perhaps some of the
"shining" garments of which Homer makes such frequent
mention were, after all, of silk, though imported.

The discovery of oriental objects at Mycenae and elsewhere, and the finding of "Mycenaean" objects far up the
Nile, have made it unwise to insist too much on the
impossibility of close contact with the East in the very
earliest days of Greece.   But the prehistoric presence
of silk in Greece is a debateable point, and I leave it
with the Homeric commentators.

Gibbon points out the curious suitability of the
Greek climate to silk-worms, and notices that until the
twelfth century, when the victorious Roger, the Norman
King of Sicily, carried off to Palermo the weavers of
Thebes, Argos, and Corinth, Greece alone of all European
countries, possessed the silk-worm.   It is, however, said
by some not to have been introduced into Greece before
Byzantine times.

The Eastern fashion of embroidering or weaving stripes
across the material is of high antiquity in Greece.   The

[54] Arist., *Hist. An.*, v., 19.
[55] *Customs and Lore of Modern Greece*, by R. Rodd. London,
Stott, 2nd Edit., 1892.

decoration of the garments on countless archaic vases testifies to the prevalence of this fashion (*cf.* The Naples terra-cotta of Fig. 7). Fringes were also largely used on the edges of garments, a fashion derived more or less from Asiatic styles.

In Fig. 45, where Penelope sits sadly at her loom, a curious pattern of winged human and animal forms is in process of production in a frieze-like band on the web. This vase is exceedingly interesting as giving a good idea of an ancient Greek loom. The threads at the bottom are held down, it will be seen, by small weights.

So far as I am aware only one set of fragments of a Greek dress, on which a pattern can be made out, still survives. It is given in Fig. 54. It was found in a grave in one of the Greek colonies in the Crimea. The decoration (human figures between floral bands) is much like what may be found on many Greek vases. In the British Museum, 3rd Vase Room, No. E 137, Case E, on a vase signed by Hieron (Fig. 55), Demeter wears a gorgeous himation covered with small figures. As the drapery becomes more graceful, after the archaic period in art, plainer stuffs as a rule come into use, depending for their effect on the hanging of their folds rather than on the pattern of the material.

As to colour, saffron seems to have been a favourite with women, together with red. Gentlemen wore white, as is specially mentioned by Theophrastus.[56] These white garments were frequently cleaned by the fuller,[57] their spotlessness being a test of good breeding. Workmen and field labourers wore grey or brown. On the white

[56] *Characters*, 7, &c., Jebb's Translation, Macmillan, 1870.
[57] *Cf.* Theoph., *Characters*, 23, 24.

Athenian lecythi, of which some fine specimens can be
seen in the British Museum (3rd Vase Room, Cases F and
41, 42) the colours of the garments are very well preserved, and can be easily made out.   From them it is
clear that very brilliant colours were often worn by the
relations of a deceased person at times when we should

Fig. 55.—Vase signed by Hieron.   Departure of Triptolemos.
British Museum.

expect to find black or neutral tints.   In fact I believe
that on the whole series of these white lecythi, of which
some thousands exist in the museums of Europe, only a
very few of the figures of mourners appear dressed in
black.[58]

[58] *Cf.* M. Pottier's book, *Les Lécythes Blancs* (Paris, 1883),
which deals at some length with the whole subject of this
particular class of vases.

The statues of the Acropolis series (Chap. III.) have garments of very noticeable brilliancy. The chief colours used are blue, red, and green. It is unfortunate that these colours are surely if slowly fading from exposure to the light and air, but they are extremely interesting both from the way in which they illustrate Greek dress and from the evidence they afford of the Greek method of tinting statues.

The *hair* of the men in Homeric times is long. They are the " long-haired Achæans." Euphorbos[59] binds his locks with gold and silver. Little spirals of gold have been found lying beside the heads of skeletons in graves at Mycenae and other sites excavated by Dr. Schliemann, which, it is conjectured, were used to encircle locks of hair, though they may be only girdle rings. Mr. Leaf[60] points out that various fashions of hair-dressing may have prevailed as distinguishing tribal marks; for example, the Thracians " wear the top-knot," &c.[61] In the account given by Thucydides of the dress of the men in early times it will be remembered that ornaments in the form of the tettix are mentioned. It used to be thought that this meant a kind of fibula or clasp in the form of the tettix, and that the Athenians chose this as a symbol of their being " earth-born " (autochthonous) and not tainted by descent from any other nation. But, in more recent times, by the aid of marbles discovered in various places in Greece, it has been found that the long hair of the athlete before the middle of the fifth century was braided in a heavy lump behind, bound round and round with bands of gold or other metal till it resembled the ringed body of

---

[59] *Iliad*, xvii., 51.   [60] *Op. cit.*, p. 82.
[61] *Iliad*, iv., 533.

the tettix, which is more properly the "tree cricket" and not the "grasshopper." Fig. 56 gives an instance of such a method of hair-dressing. Athletes often bound their hair up with a simple ribbon or fillet only. Another plan of disposing of the long hair of the men when engaged in active exercise was to plait it in one or two long tails and wind these round the head. An instance can be studied in the British Museum, Archaic Lobby, No. 209,

Fig. 56.— Athlete with his hair bound up. Olympia.

the so-called "Choiseul-Gouffier Apollo." A cast of a similar coiffure is in the South Kensington Cast Collection, Perry's Catalogue, No. 34. This long plait was often dedicated by its owner to a river or marine god at some critical moment. The companions of Patroclus sacrifice their hair at his pyre; Orestes offers his to the Inachos.[62]

In the British Museum (Mausoleum Annexe, No. 798, No. 163 in "Gr. Insc. in Brit. Mus.") is an interesting

[62] Il. xxiii., 135, and Aesch. Cho. 6.

votive tablet from Phthiotic Thebes in Thessaly, dedicated by two young men, Philombrotos and Aphtho-
netos, to Poseidon, with a curious representation of two
long straight plaits of hair (eminently suggestive of
the Misses Kenwigs), typical of the owners sacrificing
this proof of their manly vigour to the marine deity
who was supposed to have life and growth more especially
under his care.

From the time of the Persian Wars, 490—479 B.C.,
men in Greece wore their hair shorter than before, but
not too short—that was the mark of the slave. It will
be remembered that one of the things that astonished
the Persian spies at Thermopylæ was the care with which
the Spartans were seen to be dressing their long hair
before the engagement.[63]

The hair of Greek women in classical times was
arranged in an endless variety of ways, which are best
studied from the monuments themselves, as it is impossible to give any adequate idea of them by means of
illustrations. Many interesting varieties can be found
in the vase-rooms of the British Museum. The terra-
cotta statuettes (or "figurines") of Tanagra, reproductions of which, from the museums of Berlin and Vienna,
are now so universal, abound in varied methods of hair-
dressing. Similar instances exist in the terra-cotta room
of the British Museum. Young girls in Greece seem
to have worn the hair loose. In the so-called "Homeric"
hymn to Demeter, "the daughters of Celeus, like fawns
gambolling through a spring meadow, rushed down the
narrow way, holding up the folds of their lovely garments, and their hair waved about their shoulders like

[63] Herod., vii., 208.

F

saffron-coloured bloom."   Older women wore various ornaments to keep the hair in place.   Gold pins, of all sizes, for this use, are found in women's graves.   A fine specimen, in elaborate gold-work, set with a fresh-water

Fig. 57.—Hair bound with a fillet.   Coin of Syracuse.   British Museum.

pearl, rewarded the excavators in Cyprus a few years ago.   It is now in the "Gold Ornament Room" of the British Museum.   A visit to this room will, I may mention, give all necessary information on the subject of Greek jewellery.

Fig. 58.—Female head, from a coin of Syracuse.   British Museum.

The Greek fillet, or braid wound several times round the head, is proverbial as a classical head-dress.   It is given in Fig. 57 from a coin of Syracuse of the Fine Period, in the British Museum.   A similar arrangement of a cord passing five times round the hair, leaving loose

locks at the crown, appears in Fig. 58, also from a coin
of Syracuse in the same collection. Fig. 59 gives an
earlier version of the same, with one simple row of beads
keeping the hair in place.

Fig 59.—Female head, with hair bound with beads. Coin of Syracuse.
British Museum.

The "Stephane," or metal circlet rising in front and
narrowing at the back, where it was tied by a ribbon
either forming a visible bow or one concealed by a
knot of hair, was the suitable adornment of dignified;

Fig. 60.—Coin of Segesta. Hair bound with a "Sphendone."
British Museum.

noble matrons. Hera, the Queen of Heaven, generally
wears it. A fine instance occurs in the British Museum,
Elgin Room, No. 504.

Casts of similar ornaments may be found in the South

Kensington Collection, from the well-known busts of Hera in foreign museums.

The "Sphendone" (like a sling in shape, as its name implies) was a band of ornamented cloth or leather put on either from the back or front, and ending in a tie

Fig. 61.—Coin of Syracuse. "Sphendone" wound several times round the head. British Museum.

or band. Fig. 60 gives an example of the art of the Finest Period on a coin of Segesta, now in the British Museum. Fig. 61, a coin of Syracuse, also in the National Collection, shows how the long ends of the

Fig. 62.—Tetradrachm of Syracuse, with legend "Εὐμένου." Instance of a wide, short "Sphendone." British Museum.

sphendone might be wound several times round the head as a finish. In Fig. 62, from a tetradrachm signed by Eumenos in the British Museum, the sphendone is shorter and wider than in the previous example, ornamented with stars, and tied on the top of the head with a small bow. In Fig. 63 it comes lower at the back of the head, and ends in a band across the brow.

The "Ampyx" was a metal diadem or snood, of which

Fig. 63.—Tetradrachm of Syracuse, by Phrygillos. "Sphendone." British Museum.

an instance is given in Fig. 64, also from a coin of Syracuse signed by Eumenos.

The "ampyx" is sometimes worn in conjunction with the hair-net, as in Fig. 65, again from a coin of Syracuse

Fig. 64.— Coin of Syracuse. Female head wearing the "ampyx." British Museum.

in the British Museum. The two ornaments are connected by a flat buckle above the ear.

The net, with the "ampyx" reduced to a very small frontlet, occurs on the famous decadrachm of Syracuse signed by the artist Kimon, of which the Museum is justly proud (Fig. 66).

A head-dress very similar to the "sphendone" but

Fig. 65.—Coin of Syracuse. Female head wearing "ampyx," joined to hair-net by a buckle. British Museum.

more completely covering the head, called the "sakkos," from the goat's-hair cloth of which it was made, will be found in the cut (Fig. 67) also from a Syracusan coin. In archaic monuments, as, for example, in the Acropolis series

Fig. 66.—Decadrachm of Syracuse. Signed by Kimon. Hair in a net with frontlet. British Museum.

(cf. Figs. 33, 34, 35, 36,) very elaborate crimping and curling seems to have been in vogue. The forehead is covered with neatly-set wig-like locks that sometimes look almost

like snail-shells.　Long tresses that have been compared
variously to ropes of pearls or of onions are depicted in a
painstaking way, very dear to the early artist.　At a
later period much freer modes of treatment prevailed, as
our illustrations (Figs. 57—67) have shown.

A great deal has been written and said about the great
beauty of the figures of the Greek women owing to their
severe disregard of any garment at all corresponding to
the modern corset.　But there is little doubt that under
the chiton, ladies often wore a broad supporting band round

Fig. 67.—Female head wearing the "Sakkos."　Coin of Syracuse.
British Museum.

the body over the ribs or breast, ($\sigma\tau\eta\theta\acute{o}\delta\epsilon\sigma\mu o\varsigma$, " fascia pec-
toralis "). 　An instance of such a support can be clearly
made out on a vase in the British Museum (3rd Vase
Room, No. E 246, Case 29), where a lady is either
putting on or taking off her chiton at the bath.　This
band was probably stiffened in some way or made of
leather—occasionally it seems to be supported over the
shoulders by strings and buttons, like braces.　The famed
"cestus" of Aphrodite (*Il.* xiv., 214) may have been
worn next the skin, but its elaborateness suggests something that could be seen, therefore it may have been an
outer girdle.　*Cf.* Fig. 31).

In later times some kind of band was used to repress a tendency to over-stoutness.[64]

In very early vase-paintings with geometrical patterns the waists of the women are so unnaturally narrow that they have raised a suspicion of tight-lacing, even at that remote period, but as the men share in this anatomical

Fig. 68.—Fragment of a Vase, with female figures and geometrical patterns.

peculiarity it is probably due to the artist's early endeavours to portray the human form, emerging as his art was from purely geometrical forms of triangles and squares (Fig. 68).

As may be seen in Fig. 32, the "Running Girl" of the Vatican Museum wears a deep supporting belt when

[64] *Mart.*, 16, 66.

actively exercising, and at such times this must have been usual for women of all ages. The elaborate cross-girdlings to which I have referred (Fig. 25), and which remain in the popular mind as the recognised Greek style, were probably a reminiscence or repetition of a similar girdling beneath the chiton.

Sunshades occur with considerable frequency on Greek monuments, but, as in the case of the East, whence the fashion probably came to Greece, they are generally held by an attendant over the heads of persons of importance. Eros, in the Parthenon frieze (British Museum, Elgin Room, No. 324, Slab 6, Fig. 41), holds one for Aphrodite. In the Berlin Museum is a vase on which is painted a satyr advancing with mincing steps behind a veiled lady, carefully holding a parasol to shield her. On later vases of post-Alexandrine times (as for instance, in Nos. F 276, Case 55 ; F 236, Case 50-51 ; F 336, Case 12 ; F 375, Case 13, of the 4th Vase Room of the British Museum) they can be noticed in great numbers among the various adjuncts of beauty used by the ladies of the time.

In the house the Greeks seem frequently to have gone barefooted, especially in summer. This fashion was followed by philosophers who affected simplicity, by arti-sans when working out of doors, as well as by Spartans old and young. But in Athens the feet were generally covered out of doors either by sandals, or mere soles tied on with straps, or "made" boots and shoes of leather. Hunters, country-folk, and travellers wore high boots. Shoemaking is frequently mentioned by Greek authors, and various kinds of cut are spoken of as the "Laconian," the "Amyclean," and others ; but, although Greek monu-ments show an extensive variety of boots and shoes, the different kinds cannot be identified with any certainty. Fig, 69 gives a few of the varieties met with. Well-fitting shoes were a token of good breeding in Athens; mended shoes are given in Theophrastus[65] as one of the signs of avarice, over-large or nailed shoes were " boorish " except for military wear.

Ladies out of doors covered the head with a fold of the himation. On some of the Tanagra figurines outside the himation a parasol-like disc is seen on the heads of ladies, balanced in a manner impossible in reality (Fig.

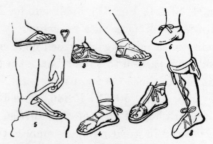

Fig. 69.—Varieties of boots, shoes, and sandals.

42). Foreign catalogues still define these discs as "straw-hats," but it has been suggested that they may be curious instances of a survival. On many of the figures found on the Acropolis an iron spike is inserted in the crown of the head (Fig. 70), in a way that seemed unnecessary and puzzling, until the view was propounded that these spikes probably supported a wooden conical disc which served to protect the fine colouring of the figures from damage by rain or birds. And so, when the artist of the smaller kind of statue, the " figurine " of Tanagra, set to work, he copied

[65] *Characters*, Nos. 14, 25.

the disc on occasions when it was no longer wanted as a
protection from the weather, and made it appear as part of
the dress of ladies of the period. Against this view it
may, perhaps, be urged that the art of the figurines of
Tanagra is too fresh to be merely a " derived" art. In
that case the puzzle of the head-dress is still unsolved.
A covering for the head for men in Greece of very general
use is the " Petasos " (πέτασος), or flat felt hat with flaps
at the front and back and over the ears, these flaps being

Fig. 71.—Varieties of the " Petasos."

sometimes tied on the crown or under the chin in the
fashion of the modern " fore-and-aft " cap. Fig. 71
gives some of the various ways of wearing the Petasos.
In later times ladies seem to have occasionally donned it
as it occurs on some of the figurines from Tanagra.
With the chlamys the Petasos is worn in Greek art by all
travellers and hunters, and therefore, by Hermes, the
travelling messenger of the gods.

Artisans and fishermen wear the " Pilos " (πίλος) a
conical cap of felt or leather. Odysseus as a wanderer
and seafarer, Charon as ferryman of the dead, and

Hephaistos as the workman god, all wear it in Greek art.

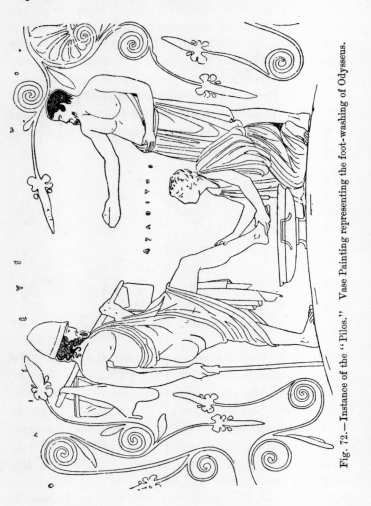

Fig. 72.—Instance of the "Pilos." Vase Painting representing the foot-washing of Odysseus.

Fig. 72 from a vase (being the reverse of the vase, Fig. 45, representing Penelope at the web), shows Odysseus in the Pilos undergoing the foot-washing at the hands of the aged attendant, Eurycleia. In Fig. 73 some sailors wear it, and in Fig. 74 it is the headgear of Hephaistos. The Pilos seems to have taken the place now filled by the skull-cap as a head covering for invalids and hypochondriacal patients. Plato[66] thus amusingly refers to the custom : " When a carpenter is ill he expects to receive a draught from his doctor that will expel the disease and get rid of it, but if anyone were to prescribe to him a long course of diet, and to order him to put little caps ($\pi\iota\lambda\acute{\iota}\delta\iota\alpha$) upon his head with other treatment to cor-

Fig. 73.—Sailors wearing the Pilos.

respond, he would soon tell such a doctor that he had no time to be ill, and wishing his physician a good morning he would enter on his usual course of life, or, should his constitution prove unable to bear up, death puts an end to his troubles."

There is little doubt that Greek ladies were in the habit of rectifying, by artificial means, any defects of complexion induced by their confined indoor life and want of exercise. In the British Museum (3rd Vase Room, Case 43) is a pot, found at the Greek colony of Naucratis, in Egypt, which still contains some of the rouge it used to hold.

[66] *Republic*, Bk. iii.

In the *Oeconomics* of Xenophon, where the whole duty of a Greek wife is set forth in most delightful terms, the bride is admonished by her husband to abjure rouge or powder, false or dyed hair, and high-heeled shoes, as, if she manages well, she will not need artificial aids to beauty, for time will not damage her influence.

These artificial additions to personal charms can, however, hardly be regarded as properly forming part of my subject. The object I had in view in undertaking the task which I have now completed was threefold. I desired, if possible, to concentrate the light already thrown on the nature and character of the dress of Ancient Greece, if not indeed to increase it; but I also had in view the necessities of those who from taking part in dramatic representations, or from other causes, wished to impersonate ancient Greeks, whether male or female. My third desire was to induce my readers to visit the National Museums to study the subject at first hand. If I have succeeded in any of these aims my work has not been in vain.

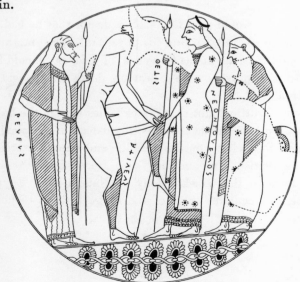

Fig. xxxviii. Athenian plate (ca. 600 B.C.) Athens National Museum. L. to r. Peleus, Achilles, Thetis and Neoptolemus.

INDEX.

G

Fig. xxxix. Artemis of Versailles. Paris. Louvre Museum. Goddess wears short chiton.

The history of the development of dress from ancient times to the present is absorbing, not only for the student of costume, but for anyone interested in fashion, for as "there is nothing new under the sun," much of our fashion design is taken from that of the past.

The costumes of ancient Greece have lent much to the styles of later ages, such as the peplum, high heels, the high standing collar of Elizabethan times, and possibly more.

Our knowledge of prehistoric Greek dress is based mainly on archaeological evidence from Crete and the mainland. Men and women and their brightly colored clothing are represented in wall frescoes, statuettes and on sealstones. The clothing of this time was very different from that of the Homeric age when men began to wear armor instead of loin cloths and the women wore the chiton and a veil-like outer wrap. Later the flowing robes of Oriental fashion were the model in the sixth century B.C., followed by the more simple Dorian dress as all things Oriental were discarded at the time of the Persian Wars. The Dorian chiton was held together by pins, and was later discarded in favor of the Ionian which was a sewn garment worn by men and women alike. This chiton was worn in varying lengths, long for sedentary occupations and short for active exercise.